Healing Family Wounds

A Practical and Compassionate Guide to
Successfully Navigating Sexual Abuse Within the Home

Shanti Duncan, Ph.D.

Healing Family Wounds

A Practical and Compassionate Guide to Successfully Navigating Sexual Abuse Within the Home

Shanti Duncan, Ph.D.

First Printing:

ISBN: 979-8-9878686-2-1

Contact author:
Shanti Duncan
12407 North Mopac Expwy Ste. 250-285
Austin, TX 78758-2475
shanti.duncan.lpc@gmail.com

working with youth going through treatment that addresses sexual behavior problems. Truly allows for life transformation and empowerment of clients. A positive read."

Collaborative Approach to Youth Rehabilitation – "I recommend this book not just to therapists or counselors who work with young adults who have sexual behavior issues, but also to anyone who is involved in their treatment and rehabilitation, who needs to get their hands on this book. Judges, probation officers, etc., would really benefit from reading this book. It goes back to the idea of "the village raising children." This book frames the successful treatment of sexual behaviors in children as a team effort."

Table of Contents

Chapter 1

Discovering Abuse

H*e is my son. I love him, and I want to help him, but if anyone else had done this to my daughter, I would want to kill them. I just don't know what to do. I'm so angry.*

We've been married for years, and we have children together. How could I be with someone and not know they were doing this? How did I miss it?

I thought we were good parents; we always know what the kids are doing and who they are with. How was this happening right under our noses?

Child Protective Services seem to think I knew about it and didn't do anything, and I'm afraid they will take my kids away. What do I do?

Suddenly, everything you thought you knew about your family, home, and life has been called into question. Your world has abruptly been turned upside down. The discovery of sexual abuse within your household—whether perpetrated by a family member or someone you trusted—has shattered your sense of safety and normalcy. The emotions swirling through you are likely intense, contradictory, and overwhelming.

You are not alone in this storm of confusion, anger, and heartbreak. Sexual abuse thrives in silence, and breaking that silence can feel terrifying. The shame and stigma surrounding this issue often leave families feeling isolated, unsure of where to turn or who to trust. But know this: by picking up this book, you've already taken a crucial first step toward healing and protecting those you love.

The good and bad news here is that you are not alone. The statistics vary depending on what research you are looking at, but according to the Center for Disease Control (CDC), about one in every four girls and one in every thirteen boys are sexually abused before they turn eighteen (Fortson et al., 2016). Some research puts the number of boys impacted by sexual abuse as high as one in six or seven. It is difficult to get firm statistics because most abuse goes unreported, and researchers often have different definitions of what constitutes sexual abuse, so the reported numbers can vary widely. There is no doubt, however, that sexual abuse of children, both boys and girls, happens with alarming and heartbreaking regularity.

We often put a lot of time and effort into teaching our children to be careful about strangers. However, more than 90 percent of sexual abuse happens from someone the victim knows, often someone they know well. Frequently, the person causing the harm is a close family member, friend, or a trusted member of the community. It is much more common to find out that a child has been abused by someone in their household or close circle of family and friends than it is for a child to be sexually abused by a stranger, though, of course, that does happen as well. Stranger abuse, however, is not the focus of this book.

"I had no idea this was happening. How did I miss it? She said she told me, but I didn't know. Do you think they will take my kids away?" A distraught mom was in my office, overwhelmed by the recent discovery that her older child had been sexually abusing her younger child for several years. Her son had just been placed in our treatment program for youth with sexual behavior problems, and she was trying to figure out how to support both her children, keep everyone safe, and make sure she was doing everything the court wanted her to do.

In her daughter's forensic interview, the little girl had told the interviewer that she had told her mom what was happening a while ago and that her mom had not done anything about it. While there are parents who deny or ignore information like that, this mom was sure that had she known, she would have immediately intervened. It turned out that the girl had told her mom that her brother was "bothering her," and Mom had then told him to leave his sister alone. She had no idea that her daughter meant more than the usual siblings annoying each other and was feeling extremely guilty that she had so misunderstood what her daughter meant to say. She was also very worried that authorities would believe she knowingly allowed her daughter to be sexually abused and would place the kids in foster care. That is one of the many reasons why it is a good idea to teach children the actual names of their body parts and talk about what to do if someone makes them uncomfortable. It is possible that if this little girl had the vocabulary, she may have been able to describe to her mom more accurately what was happening, and the abuse could have been stopped much sooner.

In the end, the court recognized that as soon as this mom realized what was happening, she called the authorities, separated the kids, and did everything she could to keep her daughter safe and get both children the help that they needed. Everyone actively participated in treatment, and they were able to develop healthy relationships with each other and move forward as a safe, well-functioning family. It was not a short or easy process, but it was achievable, and both kids were able to get what they needed to heal.

Often, when people think about sexual abuse, they imagine a stranger snatching a child from a bus stop, store, or park. I remember in my childhood being taught about "stranger danger" and being reminded to avoid walking near vans with no windows, as someone was apt to jump out of the sliding door, grab me, and speed away. It is true that children and adults do get abused by strangers. However, most people who sexually abuse children know the person they victimize and can cause harm because they come from a position of love or trust from within the family, among a circle of friends, or from working with the child (Snyder, 2000). It is also common for people to picture an adult male when thinking about someone who has committed a sex crime. Adolescents account for about 35 percent of sexual offenses against minors, and while 90-95 percent of those adolescents are male, girls and women also commit sex crimes (Finkelhor et al., 2009).

The discovery that someone you love has been sexually abused is overwhelming, and if the abuser is also someone you love and trust, it can feel like a bomb went off in your life, and you have pieces scattered everywhere. Whether it is parents who have discovered that one of their older children is abusing one of their younger children or a parent who has just discovered that their spouse or partner has been abusing one or more of their children, people are universally overwhelmed, worried, and often feel at a loss.

The non-offending parent, or parents, usually want to do everything they can to ensure their children's future well-being and safety. They often do not have people to turn to who have been through this and can give them advice. In some cases, the advice or directions of law enforcement or Child Protective Services (CPS) can feel contradictory, unhelpful, or even adversarial in nature. It is hard to know what to do and if they should trust their instincts since they may be feeling very guilty that they were not aware of the abuse in the first place.

There is no good way to find out your child is being hurt. The information is overwhelming for parents no matter if they walked in on the abuse, if they are told directly by either the person being abused or the person who is causing the abuse, if they got a phone call from the school letting them know their child told a teacher or counselor, if a family friend or neighbor comes to them with concerns, or if police or Child Protective Services call or show up at the door. There is no good scenario or way to make that news easier to hear or deal with. It is important, however, to acknowledge the situation and do what is necessary to keep everyone safe. Many people's instinct is to try to convince themselves that they misinterpreted what happened or that they are being suspicious for no reason. Ignoring abuse leads to serious consequences.

I once worked with a young man who had been abusing his younger sister over a long period of time. His parents had actually walked in on the abuse at least a year before it came to the attention of authorities and was stopped. This young man told me that when his parents walked into his bedroom while he was abusing his sister, they asked him what was going on, and he told them that he and his sister were praying together. The parents accepted this without question, and it was never mentioned again.

The abuse continued for quite a long time before the sister was able to get the courage to let someone at her school know what was happening, and law enforcement intervened. The parents' desire to pretend nothing bad was happening left their daughter enduring abuse for a much longer period of time and their son feeling unable to stop himself, despite promises to himself and his sister that he would. The damage to both children's relationships with their parents was profound. It can be difficult and overwhelming to face uncomfortable truths, but no one can heal without looking at the reality of the situation. Hoping things are okay is tempting, but it doesn't solve anything.

In this book, I will share with you the things that I have learned over the last twenty-plus years from countless conversations with worried parents and families and my work with both survivors and perpetrators of abuse. There are ways to manage the stress and logistics of parenting through this type of crisis and strategies that can help ensure that you and your children can not just survive this but end up thriving with safe, happy, and healthy lives.

TL;DR

- Discovering that sexual abuse is happening in your home is an overwhelming and often isolating experience, but you are not alone.

- Most sexual abuse happens at the hands of someone who knows the victim well—often involving people who care deeply about each other.

- Sexual abuse can be hard to talk about. It is helpful if children know the correct names for their body parts and that it is a good idea to let a trusted adult know if someone is making them uncomfortable.

- Healing can happen—for everyone involved.

- While most people picture an adult male when thinking about someone who would commit a sex crime, it is important to remember that inappropriate sexual behavior can be initiated and happen by anyone. People of all ages and genders commit sex crimes.

- It is difficult to face the reality of sexual abuse, but unless the problem is looked at openly and realistically, it cannot be solved.

Key Terms in This Chapter:

Adolescent offenders: Minors who commit criminal acts or engage in delinquent behavior. (Office of Juvenile Justice and Delinquency Prevention, 2020)

Center for Disease Control (CDC): The national public health agency of the United States responsible for disease control and prevention. (Centers for Disease Control and Prevention, 2023)

Child Protective Services (CPS): A government agency responsible for investigating child abuse and neglect reports and providing services to at-risk families. (U.S. Department of

Health & Human Services, Administration for Children & Families. Child Protective Services. https://www.childwelfare.gov/topics/responding/cps/)

Denial: A psychological defense mechanism in which a person refuses to accept reality or facts. (American Psychological Association)

Forensic interview: A structured conversation with a child conducted by a trained professional to gather information about possible abuse or neglect. (National Children's Advocacy Center. (2023). *Forensic Interviewing: A Primer for Child Welfare Professionals*.https://www.nationalcac.org/wp-content/uploads/2019/01/Forensic-Interviewing-A-Primer-for-Child-Welfare-Professionals.pdf)

Foster care: A system in which a minor is placed into a ward, group home, or private home of a state-certified caregiver. (Child Welfare Information Gateway, 2021)

Healing: The process of becoming healthy or whole again after physical or emotional trauma. (*Merriam-Webster*)

Inappropriate sexual behavior: Sexual actions that are considered improper, unsuitable, or violate social norms or laws. (National Center on the Sexual Behavior of Youth, 2022)

Intervention: An action taken to improve a situation or prevent it from getting worse. (*Oxford Languages*)

Law enforcement: The system of people and organizations that ensures obedience to the law. (*Cambridge Dictionary*)

Non-offending parent: A parent who did not participate in the abuse of their child and may or may not have been aware that the abuse was occurring. (National Children's Alliance, 2022)

Outcry of abuse: The first verbal statement about abuse made by a victim to another person. (Texas Department of Family and Protective Services, 2018)

Perpetrators: Individuals who commit harmful or illegal acts against others. (*Merriam-Webster*)

Sexual abuse: Unwanted sexual activity, often involving physical contact, perpetrated against a person who cannot or does not give consent. (American Psychological Association)

Sex crime: A criminal offense involving illegal or coerced sexual conduct against another person. (Legal Information Institute, Cornell Law School)

Stranger abuse: Sexual abuse perpetrated by someone unknown to the victim. (RAINN – Rape, Abuse & Incest National Network)

Stranger danger: The warning about the risks associated with trusting or interacting with strangers. (*Oxford Learner's Dictionaries*)

Survivors: Individuals who have lived through a traumatic experience, such as sexual abuse. (RAINN)

Treatment program: A structured approach to address mental health or behavioral issues through various therapeutic interventions. (American Psychological Association)

Trusted adult: A responsible person to whom a child feels comfortable talking about personal matters or concerns. (NSPCC, 2022)

Victimize: To subject someone to deception, duress, or other criminal activity. (*Oxford Languages*)

Well-functioning family: A family unit that effectively manages stress, communicates openly, and supports individual growth. (Family Process Institute, 2021)

Youth with sexual behavior problems: Minors who engage in inappropriate or harmful sexual behaviors toward others. (Association for the Treatment and Prevention of Sexual Abuse, 2022)

Chapter 2

Beginning to Heal – Why Getting Professional Help Matters

The echoes of sexual abuse can reverberate throughout a person's life long after the actual events have ended. But the depth and duration of those echoes? They're not set in stone. In fact, the response of those around the survivor—particularly in the crucial period following disclosure—can dramatically alter the course of healing. It happened that two clients I often saw on the same day of the week starkly illustrated the truth of the contrast in outcomes that can happen between supported and unsupported survivors.

Two clients, two stories of childhood sexual abuse at the hands of trusted adults—on paper, their experiences might have seemed similar. But as I listened to their narratives unfold, the divergence in their healing journeys became impossible to ignore. Their tales serve as a potent reminder: While we can't change the past, how we respond in the present can reshape the future.

The first person, now an adult, was abused by a family friend when she was in grade school. She was initially believed, though later told she was exaggerating and should just have gotten over it as it was not a big deal anyway. The adults around her never acknowledged the full extent of what happened to her.

Even though she was initially believed about some of what had happened, she was not given any help. Her family and community's approach was to act as if it had not happened, not discuss it, and definitely not have her meet with any mental health professionals. In fact, some of the adults around her got overwhelmed themselves and had their own trouble managing their emotions after the abuse came to light. She ended up feeling like she was the cause of problems for the adults around her and that she needed to not express any feelings or difficulties in order to help her grown-ups manage themselves.

As an adult, this client is often overwhelmed by panic attacks, nightmares, and other symptoms of post-traumatic stress disorder (PTSD). She has difficulty with personal relationships and frequently struggles with day-to-day tasks. She often reports that she dislikes herself and hates how she responds to things and how her brain works.

In contrast, often on the same day of the week, I also meet with a client who is still a child. She was abused when she was younger, about the same age as the adult client had been, for an extended period of time by a parent. After she disclosed the abuse to her mom, her mother immediately evicted the perpetrator from their home, ensuring my client never had to face her abuser again. The mom contacted law enforcement,

12

ensured that her daughter knew she would keep her safe, and repeatedly reminded her that what had happened was not her fault. She sought out mental health professionals for her daughter, herself, and her other children, and when it was clear that any of them needed a different provider or a different kind of help, she worked to get them what they needed.

My young client was allowed and encouraged to have and express her feelings about what had happened whenever she had them. This client's extended family was also aware of what happened, and all of them expressed support for her and her family. Relatives nearby came to help the mom with child care and made sure the kids had fun things to do. Relatives who lived further away sent her and her siblings comfort items as gifts. Family and friends also sent food delivery to make sure the mom not only did not have to figure out dinner every day but also to help her adjust to going from a two-income to a one-income household. My client felt embraced, believed, protected, and loved. That was not magic; she still had lots of things to work through in therapy, and the first little while was rough for her and her family, but the abuse is now several years in the past, and she is thriving. She has a great support system in place, and if she does have something happen that feels overwhelming or bothersome, she feels empowered to reach out and ask for help and confident that she will be able to handle it and that the adults around her will support her.

I do not believe that the difference between the two clients has anything to do with either of their inherent abilities to be resilient. It has to do with how people reacted to and treated them after the abuse became known. My adult client is an intelligent, talented, determined person, and I have no doubt that she will continue to work through the pain and move toward healing. That being said, if she had been allowed to process and heal from the abuse she suffered and if she had been believed and supported when she was still a child, things would likely be very different for her. She would not have had to carry that all these years later, along with the other health and well-being issues that all too often come along with having to live with unresolved trauma.

Parents I talk to are often worried that their children are irreparably broken and will never be able to have a good life. Abuse can't be erased for either the person who abused or the person who was harmed, but it is possible to have a wonderful, healthy, thriving life after abuse. It is a lot of hard work, though, and will not happen if the abuse is ignored or the people involved are told to forget it and just move on.

I have been working with both people who have endured sexual trauma and people who have engaged in traumatic sexual behavior for over twenty years. In that time, I have seen hundreds of individuals who have their own unique stories and experiences and their own journey toward healing. All those journeys start with confusion and overwhelm; many also with doubt and secrecy. In the U.S., we don't generally talk about sex, even though it is everywhere in movies, books, and media. Good quality sexual education is rare. Most adults are uncomfortable discussing sex and sexuality with children, and that is even more true when something has gone wrong.

There are a lot of good quality books and resources for parents about how to talk to kids about sex and lots of wonderful books for children with information about puberty and sex. If those books do address abuse, they mostly talk about not letting people touch you and talking to an adult you trust if someone has made you uncomfortable. There is not much in the way of

14

information for parents on what to do when they realize sexual abuse has already been happening. Books and resources for parents discussing how to help a child who is acting out sexually are even rarer than resources with information about how to help a child who has been victimized.

I have met lots of parents of children who were abused who do not want their children to participate in therapy. There can be many reasons for this, often because of the parents' lack of comfort with the subject or feelings of family loyalty, but parents mostly have the best intentions. Many parents hope that if they just pretend it didn't happen, don't talk about it, and don't think about it, their children will be able to forget about it, put it behind them, and move forward in life as if it never happened. It would be nice if we humans could do that, but unfortunately, that is not how the human brain works. A family discussion where the person who was doing the abusing promises never to do it again and the person who was being abused is told to forgive and move on is not useful and will not help anyone involved move forward in a healthy way.

It is a vulnerable feeling to talk about abuse within the family out loud, to call authorities with the knowledge that now decisions will be made about you and your loved ones by people outside the family and that those people might not make the same decisions you would have made. It can be overwhelming for parents to learn the extent of what happened and for everyone to truly face the reality of the situation. The only way to solve a problem, though, is to look at it honestly. We cannot fix or address things we are unwilling to truly see. It is scary, but avoiding things out of fear, especially something as important as addressing sexual abuse, has never once in the history of humans been a truly useful approach.

Years ago, I worked with a little girl who had been abused by her older brother. The brother had been removed and was living with a relative and participating in a treatment program. However, the family strongly felt that the younger sister should not be in therapy. They were afraid that being in treatment would require her to talk about and think about what happened and would make her feel worse and cause her more problems. They wanted to reunify and have everyone in the same household again.

For reunification to happen successfully, the person who was victimized must also have a therapist, so they ended up deciding that reunification was important enough to them to override their worries about how therapy might impact them. Of course, this little girl had already been thinking about what happened; she just had no one to talk to about it until she started therapy. Once in therapy, she was able to sort through her thoughts and feelings about her brother, how much she loved him and wanted him back in the house, and also how much what he did impacted her and her worry about being safe in the future.

It was a long road for that family. The parents, by nature, were suspicious about mental health professionals and authority figures and, therefore, tended to keep information to themselves and request that their children be secretive about things as well. Therapy is generally only successful if the participants are willing to be honest.

As time went on, the parents began to relax and trust the therapists involved, and the children were also more invested in the process. My client, the little girl, was able to process her experience and learn to let her parents know how she felt and advocate for herself when she was uncomfortable. The brother was able to learn to manage himself safely. The family successfully reunited, and as far as I know, they are still doing well today.

It took a lot of effort and courage on their part to buy into allowing treatment and probation to work, as they came from a family culture that did not trust outsiders or believe in the necessity of mental health help. In their initial determination to manage the problem entirely on their own, this family came very close to causing their son to be sent to a locked treatment facility and to lose connection and trust with their daughter. Luckily, they faced their fears about talking to outsiders and got the help they needed to get the outcome they wanted: happy, healthy children.

Sometimes, the best-case scenario is the eventual reunification of the person who caused harm and the person who was harmed, and sometimes the best-case scenario is continued separation. Which one is right for a particular family can depend on many factors, which we will discuss later in this book.

Often, if the person who was victimized is a younger sibling, they will miss and want to see their older sibling. I have worked with lots of families where everyone involved participated in appropriate therapy and treatment, and the siblings were reunited in a way that felt healing and safe for the victimized person.

That is not always the case, however, and I have also worked with families that had to make alternate living arrangements because, even after the older sibling had gone through treatment and was doing well, the younger sibling did not want contact and did not feel safe around that person. In that case, reunification is not the goal, as that would involve re-victimizing the person who was hurt.

Deciding the best path for your family and everyone involved can feel overwhelming. You are not alone; countless families have gone through this. A wealth of experienced professionals can help you and all the members of your family sort out their thoughts, feelings, and experiences until the most useful path becomes obvious to everyone involved. It is possible to have compassion and concern for everyone involved while ensuring that the victimized person, or people, get all their needs met and feel safe and comfortable with themselves and their environment.

TL;DR

- The way other people respond after the abuse comes to light can make a significant difference in the long-term well-being of the person who was hurt.

- Avoiding talking about what happened in the hopes that the victimized person can "forget and move on" does not work.

- It can feel vulnerable and overwhelming to involve legal authorities and mental health professionals in the inner workings of your family, but problems are only solved by truly looking at them honestly and addressing all the issues that are involved.

- Reunification may or may not be a good option for your family. There are a lot of factors to sort through in order to decide, and experienced professionals can help guide you. The most important factor in a decision related to

> reunification is the well-being of the person who was hurt.
>
> - Avoiding dealing with things out of fear or a desire to pretend nothing is wrong has never solved any problem and pretty much always makes the problem worse.

Key Terms in This Chapter:

Locked treatment facility: A secure care setting where residents' movements and access to the community are restricted. (California Department of Social Services, 2022)

Post-traumatic stress disorder (PTSD): A psychiatric disorder that may occur after experiencing or witnessing a traumatic event. (American Psychiatric Association, DSM-5)

Resiliency: The process of adapting well in the face of adversity, trauma, tragedy, threats, or significant sources of stress. (American Psychological Association)

Reunification: A clinical process facilitating safe contact between a sexual abuse victim and offender, typically within families, following thorough assessment and preparation of all parties. (Association for the Treatment and Prevention of Sexual Abuse, 2022)

Sexual education: A teaching about human sexuality, including intimate relationships, human sexual anatomy, sexual reproduction, sexually transmitted infections, sexual activity, sexual orientation, gender identity, abstinence, contraception, and reproductive rights and responsibilities. (Planned Parenthood)

Traumatic sexual behavior: Sexual behaviors that are developmentally inappropriate, coercive, or potentially harmful, often exhibited by children or adolescents. (National Center on the Sexual Behavior of Youth)

Victimized person: An individual who has suffered direct or threatened physical, emotional, or pecuniary (financial) harm as a result of the commission of a crime. (U.S. Department of Justice, 2021)

Chapter 3

SAFETY FIRST – Steps to Healing

Thriving after sexual abuse isn't just a distant hope—it's an achievable reality. Over the years, I have had the profound privilege of guiding hundreds of families through the tumultuous waters of recovery. Time and again, I've witnessed their journey from despair—when the very idea of "normal" seemed like a cruel joke—to a place of genuine healing, happiness, and resilience. This transformation isn't reserved for a select few; it's a path open to you and your family. In the following eleven chapters, we'll map out the crucial steps that bridge the chasm between crisis and recovery, providing you with a clear roadmap from where you are now to where you long to be.

But make no mistake—this journey isn't a sprint; it's a marathon. It demands patience, courage, and an unwavering commitment to healing. Yet, with each step forward, no matter how small, you are reclaiming power over your family's story.

The SAFETY FIRST framework we're about to explore isn't just a set of abstract guidelines—it's a battle-tested strategy forged from the experiences of countless families who've walked this path before you. Their triumphs, setbacks, and hard-won wisdom have all contributed to this roadmap for recovery.

Safety isn't just a luxury—it's a fundamental human need. When we don't feel safe, our bodies go into survival mode. Our nervous systems, ever vigilant, narrow our focus to a single priority—self-protection. In this state, growth, learning, and healing become nearly impossible. They are luxuries our brains simply can't afford when they're preoccupied with keeping us alive.

This is where our roadmap to healing comes in—SAFETY FIRST. It's more than just a catchy acronym; it's a powerful reminder of the steps your family needs to take to heal from abuse, with safety as the guiding principle every step of the way. Let's break it down:

S - Safety

A - Assess

F - Function

E - Engage

T - Treatment

Y - Yourself

F - Fear

I - Integration

R - Reunification

S - Security

T - Thrive

Each step builds on the last, creating a comprehensive path from crisis to healing. By following this framework, you're not just addressing the immediate aftermath of abuse—you're laying the groundwork for long-term recovery and growth.

Safety is the first thing to think about when the abuse is discovered. In the safety chapter of the book, we will discuss what families need to know about how to report abuse and who to report it to. It is also important to start thinking about the possibility of retaining a lawyer and the options for separating the person hurting others from those being hurt. It is in this stage that people also start getting information about the court process and whether that needs to be taken into account when making decisions about therapy options.

Assess is what comes next, after the initial dust starts to settle. This chapter will focus on some of the processes of assessing how to move forward. There may be formal assessments that need to happen, and family members can also start to personally assess how they want to proceed and perhaps start to set goals. Discussions with and between members of the treatment team may need to happen to help start setting some tentative goals for the future.

Function is the next step. In this chapter, we will discuss what might be going on as you adjust to this new reality. Until now, it may have felt that figuring out how to get everyone back to functioning was a monumental, if not impossible, task. Now the idea may seem a little more attainable. Some areas that often need thinking about are issues at school for both the child who offended and the child who was victimized. In addition, issues at work may crop up for the parent, and there may be some changes in income. As members of the family get involved with therapy and other appointments, the logistics of getting everyone to all their appointments and possible court dates also need time and attention.

Engage. Once the path forward starts to become clearer and more professionals become involved, the challenge is figuring out how to engage in both the treatment and legal process. This chapter will focus on what people are commonly worried about in relation to both the therapeutic and legal processes. Individuals are often worried about being judged and sometimes resistant to having outsiders interfere in what feels like private family decisions. Parents often worry that treatment will expose the child who offended to people who will show them how to be better criminals or expose them to information parents don't want them to have. Parents are also often worried that therapy will further traumatize the child or children who have been abused. There are also often concerns that Child Protective Services (CPS), probation services, or the court may be hostile and looking for reasons to remove children or get someone in legal trouble. It is important that despite these worries, families engage in interactions with both their own hired advocates, like lawyers, and be able to express their concerns and worries to their treatment providers.

Treatment is one of the most essential components of healing. This chapter will focus on the questions parents often have about what treatment involves and how long it might take. Often, though not always, the person who abused others is court-ordered to treatment, so there is usually not a lot of choice available about who the treatment provider will be and what the treatment process will be like. For the person or persons who were victimized, figuring out what to look for and how to choose a therapist can be a daunting task. We will discuss what is generally involved in treatment and what modalities may be available and useful.

Yourself. It is easy as a parent to put all your time and energy into taking care of your family to the detriment of yourself; in fact, that is often what society expects parents, especially moms, to do. It is important that you spend some time on yourself. It may be cliché to say, but it is true that you can't pour from an empty cup. In this section of the book, we will discuss managing your own stress, developing and leaning on support systems, and managing your own reactions to difficult information, especially if there is a pattern of multigenerational abuse and trauma in your history.

Fear. Let's face it, when sexual abuse enters the conversation, fear isn't far behind. In this chapter, we will tackle the fears that keep families up at night: What does the future hold for the person who caused harm? How will the survivors move forward? And let's not forget about you. How will this impact your own life and relationships? We'll shine a light on these shadowy concerns, helping you navigate the murky waters of uncertainty with more confidence.

Integration, or putting things back together again, may have seemed like an impossible goal in the beginning. This section of the book will talk about how to start putting your life back together again as you adjust to new legal requirements and safety rules at home—adjusting to the new normal and leaving room for growth and change.

Reunification is not always a desired or reasonable goal for families, but for some families, it is. This section of the book will discuss what is involved in clarification and reunification. We will discuss what factors help determine if reunification is a good idea and how to know if it is safe.

Security and safety are the most important factors in all the decisions made regarding responding to abuse. As families have become involved in treatment and court systems, what is necessary for security will change over time. This section of the book will talk about safely monitoring a person with sexual behavior problems and making sure that the person who was victimized feels safe and comfortable. We will also talk about continuing relationships with professionals who can support your family in the choices that work for everyone involved.

Thrive. Remember when this word seemed as distant as a far-off star? At the beginning of your journey, just getting through each day probably felt like a monumental task. But here's the beautiful truth: With time, effort, and the right support, that impossible-seeming goal has likely inched closer to reality. Now you might even find yourself daring to hope, dream, and look forward with a spark of optimism.

In this final section, learn from the real experts—survivors who've walked this path before you. They'll share their stories of life "on the other side," offering a beacon of hope and a roadmap of hard-won wisdom. What do they wish someone had told them when they were standing where you are now? Their insights might just be the light you need to illuminate the path ahead.

Dealing with and healing from abuse and struggle from within the family is a daunting task for any individual, let alone for the family as a whole. Each family member—adults and children alike—will have their individual thoughts, feelings, and needs. Many families are surprised to find that even though things felt bleak and hopeless at the beginning of the process, it is possible, even likely, that through their time, effort, and commitment to the process, they have been able to get to a place of calm, stability, joy, and connection.

TL;DR

- Recovery is possible, even when things seem overwhelming and recovery seems out of reach. It is possible for everyone involved.

- Recovery is a lot of work and won't happen quickly.

- Keeping in mind the steps involved and what the end goal is can help when things feel overwhelming.

Key Terms in This Chapter:

Child Protective Services (CPS): A government agency responsible for investigating child abuse and neglect reports and providing services to at-risk families. (U.S. Department of Health & Human Services, Administration for Children & Families. Child Protective Services.
https://www.childwelfare.gov/topics/responding/cps/)

Clarification: A therapeutic process where the person who caused harm takes responsibility and communicates this to the person they hurt (Center for Sex Offender Management (U.S.). (1999). *Glossary of terms used in the management and treatment of sexual offenders.* Center for Sex Offender Management. https://purl.fdlp.gov/GPO/gpo105631)

Multigenerational abuse: A pattern of maltreatment that is passed down from one generation to the next within a family. (Child Welfare Information Gateway, 2016)

Nervous system: The complex of nerve tissues that control the activities of the body. (*Merriam-Webster*)

Probation: A sentencing option in which instead of incarcerating an individual, the court releases the person to the community and orders them to complete a period of supervision monitored by a probation officer while abiding by certain conditions. https://www.txnp.uscourts.gov/content/definition-common-terms

Sexual behavior problems: Developmentally inappropriate or intrusive sexual behaviors that may cause harm to self or others. (Association for the Treatment and Prevention of Sexual Abuse)

Trauma: An emotional response to a terrible event like an accident, rape, or natural disaster. (American Psychological Association)

Treatment team: A multidisciplinary group of professionals who work together to provide services for a client.

Chapter 4

Safety – What to Do When Abuse Is Discovered

The day abuse is discovered in a family is a day that changes everything. While each situation is unique, the emotions that flood in are often eerily similar: waves of shock, doubt, confusion, and fear that threaten to overwhelm. For some, it is a bolt from the blue that instantly shatters their worldview. For others, it is the dreaded confirmation of a nagging suspicion they've been trying to ignore. It might explain puzzling behaviors you've noticed in loved ones or leave you utterly baffled. For many, it dredges up painful memories from their own past and the burden of guilt about seeing family history repeated in their own children. Many parents also grapple with the weight of the feelings that arise when wondering if they somehow caused or contributed to this nightmare.

Along with this maelstrom of thoughts and feelings comes the urgent question: "What do I do now?" Most of us don't have a roadmap for navigating this kind of crisis. Even when confided in, friends and family often struggle to offer truly helpful advice. In these critical moments, when emotions are raw, and the future feels terrifyingly uncertain, one guiding principle must take precedence above all else: safety.

If a child tells you that someone is harming them, even if you are unsure or think that perhaps that might not be happening, it is very important that you take the outcry seriously and make sure that the child is protected from the person they are reporting is causing harm. False accusations of abuse are very rare. It is, in fact, much more common for abuse to go unreported than for someone to falsely accuse someone else. So, if someone tells you they are being hurt, believe them and protect them.

What does keeping the person safe in the immediate aftermath of an outcry look like? If the person who has been accused of hurting the child is another adult, then that adult must immediately be made to leave the house. They can go to a hotel or motel, stay with a relative (where there are no other children), or find other arrangements, but one way or another, they should leave.

It can be a little more complicated if the person who is accused is still a child themselves. It isn't appropriate to kick a teenager or young child out or make them stay alone in a hotel. However, the person being hurt still needs to be protected. For some families, there are still options to remove the accused child from the home for the time being. That can look like having that child stay with a nearby relative or friend of the family that does not also have young children. If two non-offending parents live separately, it can look like the accused child moving in with the other parent while the child who was victimized stays where they are. For some families who have the financial ability, it can look like one parent temporarily moving into a different location with the accused child while the other parent stays with the other child or children. For some families, moving the accused child to a different location is not logistically or financially feasible. In those cases, a temporary solution is having a parent spend the night sleeping in the same room as the child who is being victimized. In addition, a door alarm can be purchased, which will make a lot of noise if the accused child leaves their room after people have gone to bed or when there is no supervision for a different reason.

The person who has been accused of causing sexual harm should not be left alone with the person they are accused of hurting or with any other child. For an adult, that means not being left alone with anyone who is a minor. For a child, that means not being left alone with anyone two or more years younger than them or someone who is particularly vulnerable for another reason. Eventually, more long-term sustainable safety rules will need to be put in place, usually at the direction of the court, but in the initial aftermath, it is important that everyone be in a safe place.

The other immediate concern is how to report the abuse to authorities. Each state in the U.S. has different laws, and those laws vary from country to country. I am not a lawyer and cannot give legal advice. In most places, at least in the U.S., it is a requirement that the abuse of a child be reported to the appropriate authorities. Generally, that is whatever agency is responsible for Child Protective Services where you live. Some people also choose to go straight to law enforcement and call their local police force to report the abuse. Some people choose to call a lawyer for advice prior to reporting the abuse. Keep in mind that many areas have a time limit for how long one can wait between becoming aware of abuse and reporting it, so it is important to report any abuse accusations quickly. Most states have a hotline number you can call to report child abuse, and some also have a website that allows you to file a report electronically.

It may be a good idea to reach out to a lawyer for advice about how to proceed as the investigation begins. Authorities will likely want to speak with the person accused of the offense and also with the child who outcried. Most jurisdictions in the U.S. have a procedure for victims to go to a forensic interview so that they are not questioned multiple times by multiple people but instead interviewed once by people trained to conduct those interviews in a way that causes the least harm possible. Depending on the circumstances, children may also be asked to go to a hospital to undergo a SANE (Sexual Assault Nurse Examiner) exam from trained medical staff. Sometimes the SANE exam can take place at the same location that the forensic interview does. These exams can feel overwhelming for children, and it is essential that the adults take the time to explain everything that is happening.

Generally speaking, court-related things move very slowly, so there may be a fair amount of time between the initial report of abuse and any legal consequences. It is crucial that during this time, parents continue to ensure that everyone is kept safe and that the victimized child or children are aware that they are supported and that nothing that has happened is their fault. In addition, especially if the person being accused is a child, it is also essential that the child knows they are loved and supported and that they, too, will be kept safe and given the help they need.

It is not unusual for Child Protective Services, or some other entity, to recommend to parents to place the child or children who were victimized in therapy with an agency that specializes in working with victims. I encourage parents to check with prospective therapists, both those working at agencies and in private practice, about their policies before choosing a therapist. Many agencies have time or number of session limits, which is not always the best choice. I have often seen victimized children who initially started working with a therapist whose agency only allowed them to work with any specific individual client for a certain period of time. The therapeutic relationship is one of the most important factors in determining if someone will benefit from therapy, and having to change therapists because of a policy can be difficult and make it harder for an individual to heal.

In addition to checking to see if the therapist has any time or session restrictions, it is also a good idea to know how the therapist, or the agency they work for, feels about future reunification. Sexual abuse typically happens between people who know each other, and when the abuser is also a child, they frequently abuse someone they are close to, like a sibling or other close relative. While not every situation is appropriate for reunification, most younger siblings I have worked with eventually very much want to have contact with their older sibling again. Some agencies have policies that do not allow the therapists who work there to participate in reunification, and again, it can be a significant loss for a child to have to change therapists in order to move toward their goal. Checking in with the potential therapist about the issue before the child starts seeing them helps preempt the problem of possibly having to change therapists in the future after they have already formed a therapeutic relationship.

The question of when the person who is being accused of the offense should start therapy is a little more complicated. If families have retained an attorney, they must make that decision in consultation with the attorney, particularly if they are thinking about starting treatment before it is court-ordered. Therapy works best if the client can be completely honest, and if court has not happened yet, that might put the client at legal risk since therapists and their records can be subpoenaed. Families who don't retain an attorney need to make sure they are aware that there may be legal consequences for their child based on what they discuss in therapy. If the family decides to proceed with starting sexual behavior problem treatment before court, other factors are important in choosing a therapist as well.

Many jurisdictions have contracts with local therapists to provide therapy for people with sexual behavior problems who are court-ordered to treatment as part of their probation. If it is likely that the client will be prosecuted, then it makes sense for them to start treatment with a provider they will likely be ordered to see later so that they don't risk having to change treatment providers partway through. In some states, therapists who work with clients who are in legal trouble for their sexual behavior have a specialized license. If you live in a state with that requirement, seeking a therapist with that credential is important. For example, in Texas, where I live, mental health professionals must become Licensed Sex Offender Treatment Providers (LSOTP) in order to work with people with sexual behavior problems. Even if the state you live in does not have a specialized license for mental health professionals who work with people who have engaged in inappropriate sexual behavior, it is important to ensure that the therapist you choose has training and experience in working with people with sexual behavior problems. It is a specialized branch of mental health, and it is not appropriate for people without the proper training, experience, and credentials to provide that kind of treatment.

Sometimes, Child Protective Services, the local police, or the district attorney decide not to pursue or prosecute a case. This creates a situation where there are no requirements for anyone involved to follow safety rules or engage in treatment. If this is the case for you, I would still highly recommend that you reach out to local treatment providers and act as if you are legally required to ensure safety and treatment. The recidivism rate for people who commit sex crimes is actually quite low, especially for adolescents. However, without the proper help and safety parameters, you risk the person who abused going on to hurt others, and you put the person who was abused at higher risk of having lifelong consequences of the abuse. Therapy can initially seem intimidating and overwhelming, but good treatment providers will help everyone involved heal.

TL;DR

- Every individual and family is unique, but the feelings of overwhelm and shock in response to sexual abuse in the family are pretty universal.

- Multigenerational abuse is common, and an outcry of abuse may remind a parent of their own experiences as a child.

- It is important that the safety of the person who was hurt is a top priority, and steps should be taken to ensure that the person who was accused does not have unsupervised access to that person or any other vulnerable person.

- It is important to ensure that you check with possible treatment providers to see if their credentials, experience, and policies fit the needs of your family.

- You may want to hire a lawyer so that you have legal advice from someone whose job it is to advocate for you.

Key Terms in This Chapter:

False accusations: Untrue allegations of abuse or misconduct, which are statistically rare in child abuse cases. (Oates, R. K., Jones, D. P., Denson, D., Sirotnak, A., Gary, N., & Krugman, R. D. (2000).

Licensed sex offender treatment provider: A mental health professional with specialized training and certification to treat individuals who have committed sexual offenses. (Texas Department of State Health Services. Council on Sex Offender Treatment. Retrieved from https://www.dshs.texas.gov/csot/)

Outcry: A disclosure or report of abuse, typically made by a victim. (Texas Department of Family and Protective Services. *Child Protective Services Handbook*. https://www.dfps.state.tx.us/handbooks/CPS/)

Recidivism rate: The likelihood of a person reoffending or engaging in criminal behavior after receiving intervention or punishment. (U.S. Department of Justice, Office of Justice Programs. (2014). Recidivism of Sex Offenders Released from State Prison: A 9-Year Follow-Up (2005-14). Retrieved from https://bjs.ojp.gov/content/pub/pdf/rsorsp9yfu0514.pdf)

SANE (Sexual Assault Nurse Examiner) exam: A medical examination performed by a specially trained nurse to collect evidence and provide care following a sexual assault. (International Association of Forensic Nurses) (Sexual Assault Nurse Examiner (SANE) https://www.forensicnurses.org/page/aboutsane)

Chapter 5

Assess – What Will Work Best for My Family?

In the aftermath of abuse disclosure, after the initial whirlwind of reporting and decision-making subsides, a critical juncture emerges—a time to pause, reflect, and reassess. The landscape of emotions and circumstances often shifts dramatically in these early days, rendering once-sound decisions suddenly ineffective. It's a time when feelings evolve, perspectives change, and the full weight of the situation begins to settle in.

Consider the case of a young girl I once worked with whose father had sexually abused her. In the immediate aftermath, she pleaded with her mother not to pursue divorce despite her mother's inclination to do so. The child's initial concern centered on her father's well-being—was he lonely in jail? Was he eating enough? Was he making friends? She peppered her paternal grandparents with worried inquiries about his adjustment to incarceration. Yet, as time passed, her perspective underwent a profound transformation. She began to truly grasp the gravity of her father's actions and the far-reaching damage he had inflicted, not just on her but on their entire family. Eventually, she found herself relieved by her mother's decision to divorce, and her anxious inquiries about her father's welfare gradually ceased.

Several years ago, I worked with an adult who had abused a younger family member. Initially, the person he victimized was clear that she never wanted to see him again and asked the rest of the family not to talk about him around her or let her know how he was doing. After a significant amount of time had passed and she had worked with her own therapist for a while, she asked her family for my contact information as she wanted to directly tell me how she was feeling. She contacted me to let me know she had changed her mind about never wanting to see him again and did want to have a conversation with him and thought she might feel comfortable with him being at large family gatherings again.

We were able to move forward and give her the opportunity to see him under circumstances of her own choosing. She wanted to tell him how she felt and ask him questions about why he did what he did and what he thought about it. The clarification and reunification process gave her the control to decide how much and what type of contact she was comfortable with moving forward.

She was able to get her needs met and to hear directly from him that he would absolutely respect whatever decisions she made about him attending family gatherings, regardless of whether she changed her mind at any point. Moving forward, he was always careful to have his own transportation when doing anything with his family so that he could leave at any point if she got uncomfortable. The key in both situations was allowing the person who was hurt to express their thoughts and feelings and acknowledge that feelings changing over time is normal and doesn't mean that they were wrong to feel how they felt at any point in the process.

There are often lots of assessments, both formal and informal, professional and personal, that happen after the abuse has been discovered. Professionals will do some of them, some will be required by law enforcement or the court, and some will be the private thoughts and feelings about what is going on that the people involved will have on their own.

℘℃℞

The Person Who Was Victimized

In some circumstances, abuse is discovered because someone walks into the room where it is taking place and catches it happening in real time. Often, abuse is discovered because the person who is being hurt lets someone know what has been happening, or there is some evidence that is found that indicates what has been happening. Occasionally, the person who is causing harm will let someone know what they are doing. In all those cases, it is common for people to ask the person who was hurt to report what they experienced. It used to be standard for the person who was victimized to have to talk to a great number of people about the situation, often being questioned by whoever discovered the abuse, the initial police officer, police detectives, district attorneys, and other lawyers, in addition to other adults involved in both the law enforcement and medical and mental health areas. That, of course, is very overwhelming for the person and often traumatizing on its own.

Luckily, in most areas, this has changed; at least it has for victims who are children. Most jurisdictions have facilities dedicated to making the process as streamlined, calm, and non-traumatizing as possible. These facilities usually have names like "child advocacy center" and are staffed by people who are trained to talk to children about trauma without further traumatizing them. Usually, after child abuse has been discovered, the parents will be directed to take the child, and often any other children in the household, to the child advocacy center for them to participate in forensic interviews. The interview will usually be video recorded and transcribed so that the child will, hopefully, not have to be questioned again by anyone else in the investigation process.

Sometimes, children are too scared or uncomfortable to talk, even in the forensic interview, and often, people who have been victimized test to see if it is safe to talk about what happened by only disclosing a small amount of information about their experiences up-front.

Often, in those cases, parents will be advised to take their children to work with an experienced therapist until they feel more able to disclose what happened during the abuse. While this type of forensic interview facility is pretty commonly available for children who were victimized, I do not believe there are many comparable situations available for adult victims.

Recently, I heard from some victim advocate groups at a conference that they were pushing to start having the same type of facility available for adults so they also don't need to be questioned repeatedly by multiple people. That would make reporting abuse less traumatizing, and hopefully, it is something that happens soon and quickly becomes widespread, as I believe it would mitigate some of the harm that happens to adult victims when they report that someone has assaulted them.

Often, in addition to the forensic interview, the person who was victimized may be asked to submit to a medical exam, usually referred to as the SANE or Sexual Assault Nurse Exam. This exam collects any physical evidence that may be present as a result of the abuse.

For some children, this exam can be very stressful and unpleasant, though some of the children I have worked with did not find it overwhelming. Whether it is overwhelming or not depends greatly on how prepared and supported that child feels and how the medical professionals involved approach the situation.

For example, the child that I referred to at the beginning of the chapter found the SANE exam mildly unpleasant while going through it, but because she felt loved and supported and because she had her mom with her and the medical professionals were careful to explain to her what was happening and get her permission for each step of the exam, it caused no additional trauma or problems for her.

On the other hand, I once worked with a young girl who was not told what the exam was, why it was happening, or what it would be like. She was dropped off at the medical facility by a foster parent she barely knew, who wasn't particularly nice to her anyway and who did not accompany her into the exam. From what she remembers, the medical professionals did not explain to her what was happening or do anything to help her feel safe, and her memory of the exam is as traumatizing for her as the abuse itself was. In fact, when I first met her, no one had explained to her why I would be seeing her and what therapy might be like. When she came into the office, she started screaming in fear as she was afraid I was either going to place her back in foster care or force her to participate in another exam. She was absolutely terrified. I have never seen before or since a person in my office who was as deeply frightened as that child was.

It is imperative that anyone—adult or child—going through a SANE exam has a support person with them if they want one and feel informed and in control of the process. It is also important that children are informed where they are going, who they will meet, and why. Had someone told that little girl that she was going to meet with someone who had toys in their office and was going to talk and play with her, I doubt she would have reacted the way she did. The stress that having an unknown, unexplained appointment caused her was completely unnecessary, and it took us months before she was able to feel safe in her therapeutic relationship with me.

Occasionally, in family court, a judge will order that a child who was victimized be placed in therapy, but most often, the victim in a situation is not forced to participate in therapy, as victims should not have required legal consequences as a result of being abused. Legal consequences are for the person who committed the crime, not the person who experienced the crime. That being said, participating in appropriate therapy is usually beneficial for the person who was victimized. Adults who were victimized, of course, can make their own decisions about being in therapy or not, though I strongly recommend reaching out to and working with an appropriate mental health professional. The impact of trauma can be long-lasting and touch many areas of a person's life and function. A therapist with experience working with trauma, and in particular sexual trauma, can be a significant support in recovery and healing.

I often talk to people who tell me that they tried therapy, and it didn't work for them. Please keep in mind that every therapist is different, and not every therapist is a good fit for every client. If you meet with someone and you don't feel comfortable, shop around for another person who is a better fit. If you do feel comfortable with your therapist but don't feel like therapy is helping you reach your goals, let your therapist know. There may be ways the therapist can adjust to ensure you are getting what you want from therapy. That may mean that you need a different technique or approach, and your therapist can help you connect with appropriate resources if that is needed. I have occasionally worked with clients who were told by previous therapists that they, the therapist, was the only person who could help them or who would get upset when asked about progress or goals or the possibility of other treatment approaches. If you are seeing a therapist who does not encourage you to give them feedback or to reach out to other providers to find a good fit, you should probably move on to someone else. The client's well-being should be the therapist's main concern, not their own ego.

For children who were victimized, the decision about therapy is most often left to the parents. I have met many parents who felt that rehashing what happened in therapy would do more harm than good, and it would be best to allow the child to "forget" what happened and move on with their lives. I have never seen that actually benefit anyone, though. Even if a person blocks out what happened or only has vague memories of the event, that information remains in their brain and body. It becomes part of the way their nervous systems react to the world. Without appropriate processing, most people will

43

continue to have negative consequences stemming from the abuse. Usually, those parents have good intentions, but avoiding therapy generally causes harm.

Outside the forensic interview and SANE exam, there is not likely to be any other required formal assessment for the person who was hurt. If the family decides to pursue reunification later in the process, a therapist will need to assess if that is something the victimized person wants or would benefit from. That is usually an informal assessment that happens in the course of therapy.

Sometimes, the person who was victimized might want to pursue other formal assessments, both for their own information and to have any diagnosis they might need for education or work accommodations. For example, I knew a young adult who was sexually assaulted during her freshman year of college. After the assault, she had a great deal of struggle, both personally and academically.

She found therapy helpful but was still struggling, so she decided to get a neuropsychological assessment done to see if there was any information that might be helpful. The assessment revealed that she had developed post-traumatic stress disorder (PTSD). That information helped her choose what direction would be the most helpful to take with her therapist and also gave her information to share with her university's disability office so that she was able to access appropriate accommodations to help her manage her studies.

ഇരു

The Person Who Caused Harm

For the person who causes the harm, it is likely that assessments and treatment will fall under the jurisdiction of law enforcement and the court system. How that looks exactly will differ from jurisdiction to jurisdiction and also depends on the individual circumstances and the age of the people involved.

The age at which a person can be held legally responsible for their behavior varies from state to state. I live and work in Texas, and currently, the minimum age at which a child can be prosecuted for inappropriate sexual behavior is ten. If the person who caused harm is below the age of legal responsibility in your area, the criminal court will not be involved. However, family court involvement is possible, especially if the family was already involved in the court or child protective system. For a child that young, the decision about what to do customarily rests with the parents or legal guardians. In most cases, it is a good idea to reach out to a therapist with experience working with young children with sexual behavior problems to figure out the best path forward.

Sometimes, adults get uncomfortable with what is actually typical childhood behavior. For example, I have had parents ask me what to do when the kindergarten teacher reports that their child has shown their private parts to another child or asked to see another's private parts. For the most part, as long as there wasn't force involved and all the children involved were the same age and found the interaction goofy or interesting rather than uncomfortable or scary, that is an example of typical developmental behavior. Those kinds of situations are usually best managed by simply reminding the child that private parts are private and not something to talk about or show to anyone else. However, there are situations when even very young children will engage in problematic behavior, such as being persistent about wanting to see, show, or discuss private parts, making peers uncomfortable, or engaging in inappropriate behavior with younger children, especially if the unwanted behavior continues after the child is asked to stop.

This should be an area of concern for several reasons. One, of course, is that we don't want that child to harm anyone or to continue that behavior when they are old enough to face legal consequences themselves. It also should be an area of concern because children that young don't generally engage in inappropriate behavior out of the blue, and it can indicate that the child is struggling because of their own exposure to something overwhelming for them. It is important that both the child and the other children around them are protected and get the help they need.

It is important to remember that while it is true that when young children engage in problematic sexualized behavior, it is usually an indication that there is a problem going on for that child, it does not always indicate that the child is being sexually abused.

Many years ago, worried parents brought their five-year-old to my office, reporting that the child was masturbating frequently and publicly, and no amount of redirecting her to not touch or rub herself, particularly in public, was making a difference. The parents and the adults at the child's school were all concerned that someone was sexually abusing her.

It took a while to sort out, and it was necessary for the parents also to have therapy sessions with one of my colleagues, but in the end, it became clear that this little girl was struggling with a lot of stress but not being sexually abused.

Her parents had a very tense relationship, and she had discovered that touching her private parts was both pleasurable and relaxing, so it was what she did whenever she felt stressed. It wasn't a sexual behavior for her, just a calming one. Her parents learned to manage their own emotions in a more healthy way and eventually got divorced, and she also learned other coping strategies for managing stress. Once stress levels decreased and the home became more stable, the problematic self-touching behavior resolved. Her parents brought her to see me years later for something unrelated and confirmed that the worrisome behavior had never reappeared.

Sometimes, even though a child is old enough to be held legally responsible for their behavior, there will be a decision not to prosecute. I have worked with families for whom Child Protective Services has chosen to close the case without forwarding it to law enforcement. I have also worked with families where law enforcement chose not to investigate or the district attorney decided not to press charges. In those situations, similar to when a very young child is involved, decisions about treatment and safety precautions are controlled by the adults involved. Well-done treatment for youth with sexual behavior problems often takes a lot of time and effort on the part of the child and the family. It can be difficult for families to complete treatment, both logistically and financially, without the added incentive of probation requirements and the support of the court system. That being said, treatment is not only useful in helping to ensure that the child with the sexual behavior problem can grow into a safe, well-adjusted adult, but it also lets the child who was hurt know that the adults take what happened seriously and are doing everything they can to keep them safe.

I remember a teenager that I worked with who had sexually abused his younger stepsister. The girl had been assaulted in the past by a different relative and told her parents and Child Protective Services that she did not want to go through the legal process again and would not testify, so the case was closed. Luckily, the family still took the situation seriously and required the young man to go through treatment and have no contact with her. His treatment process took almost three years. In the beginning his stepsister let the family know she wanted nothing to do with him and had no desire to ever see or hear about him again. She also started working with a therapist and was able to do the work she needed to do to begin healing from both what my client had done and the cumulative impact his behavior had on her, given that she had also been previously assaulted by someone else. After about two years, she asked her mom to let me know that she felt like she could have contact with my client and would like to have him attend family gatherings. She told her parents that knowing he had been putting time and work into his own treatment helped her feel that he and they took what happened seriously and made her feel that he realized the extent of what he had done.

It actually took quite a bit longer after she was ready for us to proceed with reunification, as his deep shame about what he did made the assignments he needed to do for reunification very difficult for him, and his treatment took a long time. This family had no legal or court obligation to follow up with the time, expense, and logistics of keeping the children separate, follow all my safety recommendations, and manage the financial and logistical treatment requirements for both children, but they did anyway. As a result of that, the stepsister was given the time and space she needed to heal, and my client was able to do the work to help ensure he would never hurt anyone like that again, and the family was able to be together again safely. That would not have happened if the adults had chosen to "put it behind them" and move forward as if it had not happened. The process was painful for all involved—the children and the adults—but it resulted in stronger parent-child relationships and healthier family functioning.

Similarly, it is not unusual for me to work with adults who engaged in criminal sexual behavior but were not prosecuted for one reason or another. Sometimes, these adults seek out therapy on their own as part of their own recognition of the harm they caused and their desire not to do that again. In some cases, they seek out therapy because a loved one has let them know that if they do not, they will cut off contact with them. Whatever the motivation, treatment for an adult with sexual behavior problems often takes a great deal of effort and time, even more so than treatment for an adolescent with sexual behavior problems. The decision to seek out therapy with a qualified provider is a positive one and helps ensure the safety of the people around them and their own well-being.

If the decision is made to prosecute the person who caused harm, many decisions about safety and treatment are no longer necessarily up to the individual or their adults. If the person who caused harm is an adult or considered a legal adult for criminal prosecution purposes, then that person will be involved in the adult court system. Each state has its own legal standard for what age is considered an adult for law enforcement purposes. In Texas, that age is seventeen, so if a sixteen-year-old commits a sex crime, they will likely be in the juvenile court system; if a seventeen-year-old commits a sex crime, they will be in the adult system. Those two people will likely have very different experiences. In some jurisdictions, it is also possible that someone younger than the official age of adulthood would be placed in the adult system, as there are often mechanisms to try children "as adults," depending on the type and severity of the crime committed.

The type and timing of assessments required for the person who caused harm will vary significantly depending on the jurisdiction, the case's specifics, the lawyer's requests, the judge's orders, and the approach of the particular professional providing the assessment services. There are various assessment tools on the market, each with its own strengths and weaknesses.

Some jurisdictions have offenders participate in a pre-adjudication or sometimes a pre-sentencing assessment with a therapist, and some do not. Usually, both a pre-adjudication assessment and a pre-sentencing assessment are risk assessments.

The content of those assessments will vary from professional to professional but usually involves a review of the records and a clinical interview. There may also be some other more objective assessment tools used. Pre-court assessments can be ethically challenging as some assessment tools are only meant to be used on clients who have already been held legally responsible for their behavior, so using them in pre-court assessments invalidates the results.

It is also not unusual in any given jurisdiction for there to be very few qualified mental health professionals to do both assessments and treatment, especially for juvenile offenders. That can lead to an additional ethical issue. If the same person is doing the assessment and will likely do the treatment, it is an ethically gray area to assess someone and then recommend that they be placed in your own treatment program. This can be a particularly difficult issue to avoid due to the scarcity of qualified professionals in some areas.

In addition to the above issues, everyone needs to remember that risk assessment tools, for the most part, were developed to be used as a treatment and research tool, not as a court tool. They aren't as reliable and valid as we would like. It is very important that no decisions be made about an individual based solely on using any one individual assessment tool. Of course, if the person is not honest in their assessment, that will also render the assessment less useful. However, before adjudication and sentencing, it is not always in the best interests, legally speaking, for a client to be totally honest about their behavior. If an individual is engaging in a pre-court assessment, everyone must understand the legal risks and how the assessment will be used. If possible, the individual's lawyer should be the one who advises them about participating or not in those types of assessments.

Sometimes, the individual's lawyer will request that the individual undergo an assessment, which may or may not include a polygraph exam. Since that assessment falls under the umbrella of the lawyer's work product and is therefore covered by their confidentiality, it can be very protective for the client. If the lawyer feels the results of the assessment would be harmful to the client, they can just not present them in court, which is not the case if the assessment doesn't go through the lawyer since, in general, mental health professionals can be subpoenaed.

Even if it is the same mental health professional, if the assessment is at the request of the lawyer, the results and any other related information belong to the lawyer, not the therapist doing the assessment, and is therefore not ordinarily subject to subpoena because of the standard of privilege that lawyers have, which is different from what therapists have. This is one way that the individual, their lawyer, and their family can get information about possible risk levels and what type of treatment will likely be the most helpful without posing as much legal risk to the individual.

It is important to remember that the rules that govern lawyers and legal procedures vary from state to state, and I am not a lawyer and cannot give legal advice. Seeking out a qualified lawyer in your area is the best way to ensure you are working with someone who knows the rules and norms for you and your family.

A common assessment question is the level of risk. Judges, lawyers, probation officers, parents, and other community members often want to know how much risk any individual poses to the community. It is a difficult and complicated question to answer. If most of what you know about people who commit sex crimes comes from TV shows and news media, then you likely believe that anyone who engages in illegal sexual behavior is very likely to do it again. Research shows us that this isn't actually accurate. Sex offenses have a lower re-offense rate than many other categories of crime.

It is a little tricky to know the exact number of re-offenses for several reasons. One is that not every crime committed gets reported; another is that different areas of jurisdiction have different names for similar crimes; and also because different researchers measure re-offenses in different ways. Some research studies have looked at crime as a whole, so if the individual who committed a sex crime goes on to commit any other type of crime, like shoplifting or drunk driving, in the future, that is listed as recidivism. Other researchers define re-offense as measuring those who commit an additional sex crime after their original conviction.

When I think about the risk of re-offense, I tend to think of the second category, sexual re-offense, more than overall crime as a whole. Either way, the recidivism rate for people who commit sex crimes is pretty low, and for adolescents, it is even lower.

Of course, the lower the recidivism rate, the better it is for community safety. Ironically, low re-offense rates do make research about what contributes to the risk of reoffending a little difficult, though. The level of re-offense is so low for adolescent offenders that it can be hard to find a big enough sample of research participants to really get good, accurate knowledge about what measurable factors play a role in risk.

Despite that uncertainty, several risk assessment tools are available on the market. Some are dynamic, meaning they measure factors that can change over time, and some are static, meaning the factors measured are generally not changeable. What type of risk assessment any individual client will be required to do depends on what is typical for the jurisdiction the person is in and the specifics of what the judge and lawyers request.

A comprehensive risk assessment commonly involves some clinical interviews with the client themselves and, if they are a minor, with their adults. In addition, whatever assessment tool or tools the provider decides is the most appropriate, often along with a polygraph exam.

In addition to risk assessments, people who commit sex crimes are often required to undergo a variety of other assessments, the details of which vary, of course, based on jurisdiction and individual needs. Often, people on probation are required to do a screening for substance-use disorders, and depending on the results of that, an individual may be required to complete substance abuse treatment as well.

Some individuals may be asked to submit to assessments that measure areas of sexual interest and arousal. While on probation, individuals are often required to submit to drug testing, as it is frequently a probation requirement that people abstain from drug and alcohol use. Some probation departments also use their own risk assessment tools, which are administered by the probation officer during office meetings.

TL;DR

- Thoughts and feelings about the best course of action may change over time.

- There are many types of assessments, some formal and some informal, that may be requested or required.

- Information gathered before a client who is being prosecuted goes to court may be used against them in the court process, so it is important to get advice and guidance from a lawyer.

Key Terms in This Chapter:

Adjudication: The formal giving or pronouncing of a judgment in a legal proceeding. (*Legal Dictionary*)

Child advocacy center: A facility designed to provide a child-friendly, safe environment for forensic interviews and services for children who may have experienced abuse. (National Children's Alliance definition)

Dynamic risk factors: Characteristics or circumstances that can change over time and may affect the likelihood of reoffending. (Andrews & Bonta, 2010)

Legal privilege: Legal protection that keeps certain communications confidential. (American Bar Association)

Polygraph exam: A procedure that measures and records several physiological indicators while a person answers questions. (American Polygraph Association)

Pre-adjudication assessment: Evaluation conducted before legal proceedings to assess risk and treatment needs. (Legal/Clinical composite definition)

Pre-sentencing assessment: Evaluation conducted after conviction but before sentencing to inform court decisions about appropriate consequences. (Legal/Clinical composite definition)

Risk assessment: Structured evaluation to determine the likelihood of future problematic behavior. (Association for the Treatment and Prevention of Sexual Abuse)

Static risk factors: Historical or unchangeable factors used to assess risk of future behavior. (Andrews & Bonta, 2010)

Work product: Materials prepared by or for an attorney in preparation for litigation. (*Black's Law Dictionary*)

Chapter 6

Function – How to Manage All the New Requirements

"I never thought I would get to this place, but now it feels like things have become pretty manageable, good even. It will get better for you, too."

Aparent whose child had been in our treatment program for many months tried to reassure a new parent who was attending their first parent group meeting. The new parent was worried about managing all the requirements and concerned that if they dropped the ball on anything, their child would face legal consequences or Child Protective Services (CPS) would take them away. The more experienced parent, now looking back on how they had felt in the beginning, was a little surprised at the progress that had already happened for them and their family and happy to be able to help the new parent maintain hope.

It is difficult to overestimate how overwhelming the first few days, weeks, and months are after the abuse has been discovered. There is a lot of uncertainty, both because parents don't know what to do but also because a lot of information needs to be gathered and decisions made by others before many of the decisions parents need to make can even be contemplated.

Most families do not go into this situation with much or any previous experience dealing with sexual behavior problems, and this is often the most overwhelmed and frantic they have ever felt. They are often interacting with professionals who are very familiar with similar situations and for whom, rather than being the focal point of all their attention, it is just a Tuesday at work. That can add to the frustration as it can feel like major decisions about you and your loved ones are being casually approached by others. Sometimes, things happen very quickly, but often, the wheels of the criminal justice system grind slowly, and the waiting and uncertainty can be overwhelming for the people involved. If the person who caused harm is an adult, the legal process can be dragged out for years. It is usually faster, though often still not particularly fast, if the person who caused harm is still a child and in the juvenile justice system.

Even if it doesn't feel like it will, time passes, decisions are made, and a "new normal" emerges. Eventually, authorities decide if the case will be prosecuted, judges make rulings about who can and cannot have contact with each other, and decisions are made about how much and what kind of treatment is necessary. Your own shock and overwhelm begin to fade, and the tasks of getting through day-to-day life start becoming more manageable.

ℰℭ

The Parent or Guardian

When parents find out that one or more of their children are being harmed, especially if at the same time they find out that the person causing the harm is also their child or perhaps an adult they had trusted, feelings of guilt and shame can be pretty overwhelming. Childhood abuse is often a multigenerational problem, and it isn't unusual for parents to have promised themselves to protect their children from experiencing what they went through themselves. When it is discovered that despite their protective goals, their children have been abused or are abusing others, the overwhelm is not just about what has just been discovered but also about the memories of the past that may be invoked.

The myriad of things that need to happen after the initial outcry, along with the sense of overwhelm, can make it very difficult to step back and look at the big picture. There are a lot of moving parts and adjustments that will often need to be made in order to accommodate safety, legal requirements, and the well-being of everyone involved. It is important to remember that you are one of the people whose well-being is important. In their worry about their children, parents sometimes forget to look after their own well-being as well. Humans have a hard time with change, and this is typically a time of significant change. Usually, one of the biggest areas of struggle for parents is the logistics of everything that needs to happen.

Often, when abuse first comes to light, people feel like they will do anything to get their children the help that they need. That isn't a bad thing, but it is also important to be realistic about logistics. For example, I often talk with families who live very far away from my office but decide they want their child to be in therapy with me. Treatment for sexual behavior problems can take years, and so can therapy for someone who has experienced trauma. In the immediate few weeks after the problem is discovered, it may seem reasonable to drive many hours to see a therapist, but that gets old and inconvenient after a while. Years ago, I worked with a teenage boy who was court-ordered to treatment from a county that is about a two-hour drive from my office. The parents were prominent in their community and, I believe, wanted a therapist who had no connections to anyone they might know. Several qualified, excellent therapists were in their area, but they were insistent that they wanted their son to see me. For reasons that I still don't totally understand, the probation officer was fine with that decision, so I became that young man's therapist.

A four-hour round-trip drive for a therapy session is a lot; predictably, they were often late or missed appointments. They eventually did transport him often enough for him to complete his treatment, but it would have been a lot less stressful and problematic for everyone if they had chosen a therapist closer to home. Ironically, when reprimanded in court for how long treatment was taking for their son, the parents complained about the difficulty of predicting traffic and getting to my office, though when they started, they repeatedly told me it would be no problem at all for them, despite my expressing a lot of misgivings. Do yourself a favor. If it is possible to choose treatment providers and other professionals who are conveniently located for you, please do so. There are circumstances when that really isn't possible, unfortunately, and I have had clients who felt compelled to come to my office from many, many hours away, but whenever possible, please don't choose to make your life more difficult. This is hard enough as it is without adding more struggle.

Many forms of abuse are multigenerational, and sexual abuse is no exception. It is not unusual for the parent of a child in treatment for sexual behavior problems to have their own history of having been sexually abused by other older members of their family as well. It is also not unusual for the abuse in previous generations to have not been acknowledged or addressed and for the people involved to have gotten very little, or perhaps no, help or support. I highly recommend that all adults involved, especially if you have your own abuse history, seek out therapy for themselves. It can also be important to let your child's treatment provider know that you have those experiences in your history so that they can be mindful of that when discussing things with you.

Not that long ago, I was meeting with the parent of one of the teenage boys in our treatment program. The young man had been in treatment for a few months at that point and was making good progress. He had also started to be more honest about his past behavior.

His mom let me know that while she did want to know the outline of what happened so she could be sure she was keeping everyone safe at home, she did not think she could handle knowing all the details. She had started working on her own trauma with her own therapist and had realized that some of the information was overwhelming for her.

Once she communicated her boundaries, we were able to focus our discussions on the essential information she needed to chaperone her son safely—nothing more. This targeted approach helped her become a more effective parent while working through her own trauma with her therapist at a manageable pace. Breaking the cycle of multigenerational trauma requires patience; rushing the process generally creates additional harm rather than healing.

Sometimes, the multigenerational abuse isn't necessarily sexual in nature but still has a significant impact on everyone involved. Years ago, we had a teenage boy in our program who had been sexually abusing his sister. He was determined to get help and not cause more harm and did quite well in treatment. His family as a whole struggled quite a bit, which caused a lot of struggle for him.

His parents certainly meant well but were harsh, controlling, and demanding. Neither of the parents wanted to interact much with any of his treatment team if they could help it, and they were not open to the suggestion of finding therapists of their own. The father once told me that while he was growing up, his father regularly and severely beat him throughout the entirety of his childhood. He was very proud of himself as he had been determined never to lay a hand on his children, and he had been able to follow through with that. That was indeed very admirable and a lot of work on his part.

Unfortunately, while he did refrain from passing down the physical abuse that had been manifest in the family for generations, he was unable to see that he did pass down the controlling, harsh, emotionally abusive parenting style that he had grown up with. I never had any doubt that this man loved his children and wanted the best for them, but his own trauma left him unable to see the forest for the trees, and sadly, he continued a legacy of pain and dysfunction that left both his children struggling. I know for sure that isn't what he wanted.

Worrying about being judged, a family culture that values family loyalty and not allowing outsiders to know your business, and the overwhelming fear that can come with realizing your children are in pain is a powerful and often debilitating combination.

It can be helpful to take a breath, remind yourself that doing the same things that you have always done will lead to the same results, and try to keep in mind the possibility that most mental health and other professionals truly only want good things for you and your family. In their strong fear of being vulnerable or judged by the therapists involved in their son's case, the parents ended up creating the very situation they were trying to avoid.

Parents also need to keep in mind the logistics of not only whatever court-ordered treatment and assessment appointments are required but also court dates, the therapy appointments for the child or children who were hurt, their own personal therapy appointments, handling school and extracurricular activities, the logistics of managing safety rules if the children are siblings or close family members, possible changes in custody and parenting decisions, possible changes in marital status, possible changes in employment and, particularly if the person who caused harm is the other parent, a possible change in income. It is a lot to juggle, and more information about managing all of that is in Chapter 9.

ဆဝ૬ૹ

The Person Who Was Victimized

In some ways, decisions about the person who experienced harm are the easiest because, frequently, those decisions are almost entirely left to the parents, and you are often not waiting on a judge or district attorney to make a decision. That is not always the case, though. Sometimes, Child Protective Services or a judge decides where the child can live and who they can have contact with. Often, however, as long as safety considerations are being followed, non-offending parents get to make most of the choices. That also means that unless you reach out to professionals for support, you may not get much advice or guidance about the most helpful thing to do. One of the reasons I decided to write this book is the number of overwhelmed parents I have met in my office and on the phone who are just trying to figure out what to do next with very few helpful resources to draw from.

As I discussed earlier, there are parents who want to avoid putting the victimized child in therapy, often feeling like it would be better to just let them forget and move on as if nothing happened. This is not a good idea. Ignoring trauma and pain has never been a way to heal it. If your child broke their leg or was diagnosed with diabetes, deciding to just ignore it and move forward would not only be detrimental but would also be considered medical neglect. Just like it is not possible for a child to heal themselves of major medical issues, it is also not a good idea to try to heal trauma by just ignoring it. The popular saying, "Time heals all wounds," isn't particularly accurate. It would be nice if that were true, but research and experience tell us it is not. Taking the time to locate a therapist who has experience working with kids who have experienced sexual trauma and who is a good fit for you and your child is worth the effort, even if it can feel very scary at first.

Children commonly experience different reactions to having been abused at different times in their lives. I remember a young girl I worked with who had been sexually abused by an adult when she was around three or four years old.

At that time, she did not think of the abuse in terms of sexual behavior, as that wasn't the way she viewed the world. She experienced the abuse as weird and icky and uncomfortable. She processed her experiences through play therapy and was able to move on.

Years later, I met with her again for a little while because once she started puberty and had a more nuanced understanding of what had happened to her, it impacted her in a way it hadn't when she was little, and she needed to work through how she felt about that.

That doesn't happen to all abuse survivors. However, one of the benefits of establishing a good therapeutic relationship with a mental health provider is that the child knows that even if they are no longer seeing a therapist regularly, they can reach out for help if they ever feel that they need to.

In addition to seeking out therapy, families also often struggle with decisions about school and other activities. If the abusive person is a sibling, close family member, or even perhaps a neighbor, they may be attending the same school and be involved in the same extracurricular activities as the child who was hurt. In some situations, this can be managed, as activities and schools often keep different age groups separate, and the children may not have much contact with each other anyway. There are times, however, when it can be very problematic.

I have worked with families who were very involved in religious activities, and youth group and youth retreat events were among the situations that posed a great deal of logistical trouble. In general, if someone needs to not participate in an activity, change schools, or otherwise make accommodation for the situation, it should, whenever possible, be the person who caused the harm. The victimized child should not feel inconvenienced or be punished for having had a bad thing happen to them.

That is also true of family gatherings and events, which can often cause a lot of logistical difficulties. If the person who caused harm is an adult, it is usually easy enough to ensure that they are removed from activities. It is often more complicated if both people are children, though.

The logistics of school and other activities are one thing, but there is also the question of who gets to know about what has happened. Sometimes, there isn't that much choice, especially if you live in a small town or a close-knit community.

Most sexual abuse crimes do not end up being in the news, but on occasion, they do. Journalists are usually pretty careful about not identifying people who were the victims of sex crimes and also not identifying minors who have committed crimes, but there are cases when the details of crimes that make the news make it obvious who the people involved are.

There are times when the circumstances also make it impossible for anonymity to be maintained. For example, I have worked with families where the abusive person was in a leadership position in the church the family attended. In those cases, the entire community knew all the members of the family, and the arrest and removal of the person who caused harm made what had happened pretty obvious to the community.

Some families I have worked with have been embraced and supported by their communities and feel comfortable with the idea that others know, at least a little, about what happened to them. That isn't always the case, and often, the person who was hurt feels uncomfortable around others who may have an idea about what happened to them. Those feelings can also change over time, and the person who was hurt should have, as much as possible, the ability to decide for themselves what they want to do about involvement in any of the community activities they had been previously involved in. Whenever possible, the person who was hurt should have control of their story and the power to decide who knows what happened and how much of the details of what happened others know.

Along the same lines, it is often important that some people involved in the child's life know what happened, though rarely is it necessary to share all the details. Many families I have worked with choose to let the school counselor know that the child has been abused.

It can be very helpful for the child to know there is an adult they feel comfortable with at school who is aware enough to help them if something overwhelming happens. For example, a child I was working with who was in middle school noticed she was having a strong, uncomfortable reaction when one of the counselors came into her classroom to talk to the students about safety, which included a discussion about good touch/bad touch.

She and her mom had met with the school counselor assigned to her at the beginning of the school year, and she knew she was able to excuse herself and go to that person's office who gave her the space she needed to both step away from the bothersome discussion and get the support she needed to recover.

That resource, and the fact that all the adults involved listened to her when she told them what she needed, meant that she only had to step out for a little bit and could return and handle the rest of her school day with no problems.

It is very important that the adults involved listen to the child and believe them when they express being uncomfortable or not wanting something to happen. In a previous year, that same student, along with all the other students, was required to go to the school nurse, who was screening all the students for scoliosis.

She was told to lift up her shirt so her back could be examined. She told the nurse she was not willing to do that and that it made her uncomfortable. Unfortunately, instead of taking her feelings seriously and calling her mom as the child requested, the nurse required that she lift her shirt despite her objections.

After that happened, she was able to go to the counselor for support and contact her mom, who came to the school to help her. However, since she had been forced to lift her shirt for the nurse despite her protests, she had a much stronger reaction and needed much more time and support to recover from the incident, which continued to occasionally resurface when other things happened that reminded her of the original abuse she endured.

No one should be forced to allow someone access to their body, especially after they have said it is not something they are comfortable with, no matter what their history is. For abuse survivors, that dynamic is particularly painful. It can be a strong reminder of not being able to have control over what was happening to them while they were being abused.

☙❧

The Person Who Abused

The age of the person who caused harm significantly impacts what requirements that person will have if the court becomes involved and also what is important to keep in mind in terms of logistics overall. If the person who abused is an adult, it will likely be required that they leave the household and have no contact with the children involved.

Even if that adult is not prosecuted, it is likely that Child Protective Services will react if the adult remains in the household with the child. I have worked with many children who are in the foster care system because they had been abused by an adult in their home, and their mothers chose to stay with that person rather than protect their child.

The decision to continue to be in a relationship with a person who has abused their child and allow that person access to their child usually results in authorities recognizing that the parent is not protective, and the child often gets removed from the home and placed in foster care.

That is not to say that reunification can never happen in a family when the person who caused harm is an adult. It certainly can. However, initial separation and a great deal of treatment and support for all members involved need to happen before it can be determined if reunification is both safe and in the best interest of the person who was harmed.

I have known families that are able to handle the situation appropriately and safely, even when the goal is to stay together.

I once worked with a family where the stepdad was inappropriate with the oldest daughter.

To his credit, he realized he had acted badly, and he let his wife know what he had done. They reported it to the appropriate authorities. Law enforcement, or perhaps the district attorney, chose not to pursue the case, and technically, the family had no legal obligation to follow any safety precautions or participate in any treatment.

The mom was a protective parent, and it was decided that the stepdad would move out for a while and pursue sexual behavior problem treatment with a local provider. Mom also sought out therapy for the daughter, and she became my client.

The stepdad did well in treatment, and after processing what she went through, my client expressed a strong desire to have the family reunite. The stepdad's therapist and I coordinated clarification and reunification, and the family was able to move back in with each other in a way that felt safe and comfortable for everyone involved.

It is often the assumption of most people that if the person who caused harm was one of the parents, the only appropriate response is for the parents to divorce and for the offender to no longer be a part of the lives of everyone else. Sometimes, that is indeed the only reasonable option and the only way to ensure the safety and well-being of the rest of the family. It is not, however, always the only viable option, as it is possible for some families to stay together in the long run without sacrificing the well-being of anyone. Whatever the long-term goal, it is important that the well-being of the person or people who were hurt is the most important factor.

For example, I have worked with a family where the father abused a child who was a part of his wife's family. He was required to leave the household and not have contact with any children, including his own, though they were not involved in the abuse, while he was on probation.

The father was in my treatment program; he did well and, after many years, was able to reunify with his children and eventually move back into the household with them and his wife. The person he hurt was, by then, an adult, and she contacted me to let me know that she was very glad he and his wife had maintained their marriage and that she could tell by the way his kids talked about him that he had become a much better father and husband and she was glad he was in their lives.

She also let me know that even though she was very happy that he had done all the work he had done to become safe, she had decided that seeing him herself was not something she wanted to do. Unfortunately, a relative had incorrectly informed her that she had to be willing to meet with my client in order for him to get permission to move back home and be with his kids.

She had called me to let me know that if that was required, she would be willing to, as it was important to her that he be able to be home with his wife and kids, but that she was worried about how hard it might be on her. I reassured her that the most important thing was that she never be uncomfortable and that there was no reason for her to have contact with him unless she wanted to. She, of course, has zero obligations to do anything she didn't want to do.

She was aware that if she ever wanted to ask him questions or tell him how she felt, I was happy to help with that, but if not, that was totally fine, too. My client has been careful since then to never attend a family gathering that the person he victimized was planning on going to and to make sure that all the relatives know they should never put any pressure on her about contact with him. That family has kept in touch with me over the years, and things have continued to go well. Everyone involved feels comfortable with how the family structure ended up.

Over the years, I have worked with many families that chose to work toward staying together, even after one of the parental figures had abused one of the children. If that is the goal, it is still important that the person who caused harm is removed from the household for a period of time and has no contact with the child or children involved. It is also important that everyone involved participates in therapy and that the child who was hurt has a therapist they are comfortable with and who can advocate for them.

That can help ensure that the child is not just agreeing to have the adult back in the household to make the other family members happy but that it is something that they truly feel comfortable with and will truly cause them no harm. Of course, the person who caused harm must also be willing to go through treatment, take complete responsibility for their behavior, and be willing to maintain a safe, responsible life and engage in healthy, appropriate relationships. If all that happens, it is possible that the family can stay together in the long term in a way that is beneficial for all. It is, however, much more common for separation and divorce to happen if the person who abused the child is a parent or parent figure. It is very important that everyone keep in mind that even if reunification is the goal, it is not always feasible or beneficial, and continued separation may end up being the ultimate and best outcome after all.

When the abuser is a parent, the non-offending parent can often feel like others view them with suspicion. Many parents tell me that they felt law enforcement and Child Protective Services were judgmental and assumed that they knew about and allowed the abuse to happen.

One mom I talked to told me that when she told the prosecutor that she wanted her husband to get probation instead of prison time so that he could continue to work and have income to help with bills, she was treated as if she were not a protective parent and would allow him to hurt the children again. She was, in fact, an extremely protective parent, and as soon as she became aware of the situation, she went to great lengths to keep her kids safe.

For her, part of keeping them safe was ensuring that they could stay in their home and their schools and that she could be available to them, which would have been exceedingly difficult if she had had to try and replace his income on her own. In addition, she knew that if he was on probation, he would be ordered to treatment and could get some help, which is what her kids wanted for him, whereas if he had been sent to prison, he would not have received sex offense-specific treatment.

In some states, treatment is available to prisoners in the system, but that is not the case in Texas. Instead of feeling supported and helped by the system, as the victims in this case, the mom and her kids felt attacked and judged, which increased their sense of overwhelm and isolation and their feelings of distress.

While some adults who commit sex crimes do go directly to being on probation, many spend some, if not a lot, time in jail or prison. Someone who goes directly to probation may be able to maintain their employment, though that depends on their job type. Most people who spend significant time in a locked facility will lose their jobs.

Even if employment is maintained, if the family had previously lived together and now one person has to live elsewhere, this will invariably add bills and logistical complications to their lives. A large part of figuring out how to function again is taking a realistic look at how to manage bills and other issues in the new normal.

Many jurisdictions have victim services departments, and often, speaking with a caseworker there can help people sort through what they need to think about and what support is available to them. This is an overwhelming process, and you don't need to do it alone.

If the person who caused harm is a child, the logistics of handling the situation are quite different from when it is an adult. It may seem obvious to say, but children are not little adults, and children who commit sex crimes are not little adult sex offenders.

When treatment for people with sexual behavior problems was first developed, the little bit of research that existed about adults was assumed to apply to children as well, and many treatment programs had shame-based programs that we now know don't work well for adults, let alone children.

Luckily, as time has passed, more research has been done, and we have a much better idea of what is actually helpful for both adults and children. It will hopefully come as no surprise to most people that children, including children who engage in hurtful and criminal behavior, are still children who need all the nurturing and activities that other children need.

The initial logistics of separating the person who caused harm from the person or people who were harmed can be more complicated when everyone is a child. While an adult can be told to leave the house and figure out how to manage on their own, a child cannot.

If the child who caused harm is in the criminal justice system, decisions about where they can live and who they can have contact with often depend on a judge. Sometimes, the judge or other authority will allow the family to remain together in the house, but most often, the child who caused harm is required to have no contact with the person or people they hurt, at least for a period of time.

That can make the logistics of managing appointments and school activities complicated. If the child is ordered to a residential treatment facility for a period of time, the logistics of school and appointments are all handled at the facility. Parents will need to manage visits and perhaps be available for family therapy sessions.

Once the child is released from the facility, some logistics will be involved in transitioning them back into the community. Often, both the parents and the child are surprised to learn that the child will be required to continue participating in outpatient "aftercare" with a treatment provider after they have successfully completed an in-patient program. The main reason for this is that it is important that the child get to practice living in a safe, responsible, low-risk way while being a part of the community, which is not something they can work on while in an inpatient setting.

The logistics can get quite complicated and overwhelming for the family. However, it is crucial that the well-being of the person who was hurt is always a priority. I have worked with hundreds of families where an older sibling sexually abused a younger sibling. In the vast majority of those cases, the younger sibling gets to a point in their own healing where they very much want to have contact with their older sibling again. Sibling abuse cases often end up with some form of reunification happening. However, even though that is usually the case, it is not always. I remember one little sister, for example, from a family where reunification was not a reasonable goal.

The older brother had been placed in a residential treatment facility, and when he came close to completing the program, the judge had to decide where to place him when he got released. The hope of the facility and the judge was that he could return home as there were no other viable relatives or places for him to go. Unfortunately, the family had avoided getting the little sister a therapist up until the point when the judge made it clear they needed to, as the brother was supposed to be released in a couple of months.

I ended up being the little sister's therapist. I was told that the goal of her being in therapy was to be able to bring the brother home. This girl, however, was terrified of him. She was under significant pressure from her parents, who wanted everyone to be together under the same roof. Even the judge and probation officers were pushing for that outcome, as no one could think of anywhere else for the young man to go.

It is imperative that the therapist for the victimized person advocates for that person's well-being, regardless of any outside pressure. This was one situation where reunification would have been harmful, not helpful, and despite creating a significant number of logistical complications for everyone else involved, the only metric important in making decisions about reunification is the victim's well-being.

Ultimately, continued separation was the only reasonable goal for this family. It is possible that as the little girl gets older, perhaps even after she reaches adulthood, she may feel differently and eventually end up being in a place where reunification is a benefit for her, but when I knew her, it definitely would have only caused her harm.

Most often, at least in the area where I live, children who commit sex crimes are court-ordered into out-patient treatment programs. That means they will participate in treatment but still live at home and attend the local school. Some parents I have worked with have been apprehensive about stigma at school and have chosen to homeschool their children when they are placed on probation.

In general, I do not recommend that. While there are some school districts that handle information about a child's legal involvement poorly, most are very discrete and can often be helpful. Children need to socialize and benefit from being able to participate in extracurricular activities at school. In addition, often children who engage in inappropriate sexual behavior struggle with social relationships with peers, and it is important that they have the opportunity to work on their ability to make and maintain friendships and appropriate romantic relationships.

If a child has been used to a school setting and is abruptly removed to be homeschooled, it can make things more complicated for both them and their family. That said, different families need different solutions, and sometimes, a change can work out well. I used to work with a young man who was nearly done with high school when he got in legal trouble for his behavior. His school district did not want him to attend the school he had been attending, though his offense didn't happen at school, and there was no reason to believe that his classmates would be in any danger.

His parents did not want him to attend the alternative school that the district wanted him to go to. He completed his high school credits through a mixture of online classes and classes at the local community college, which allowed him to not only graduate from high school but also get ahead in college credits at the same time. He was attending some of the college classes in person, and he was working, so he was able to continue to meet people and work on practicing being healthy in his relationships with others.

There are situations when the child who caused harm is not required to be removed from the home. In that case, it is still very important that safety be a top priority. In the first few days, parents often tell me that they have the child who had been hurt sleep in their room with them so that they are protected overnight. That can be helpful in the beginning, but usually isn't a good long-term solution.

It is important that the child who caused harm is never left alone with the person they hurt or any other children who are two or more years younger than they are or are particularly vulnerable for some other reason. That is logistically difficult when everyone is in the same household. This means that during daytime hours, if a parent needs to leave the house or even go into the other room, the child who has to be supervised needs to go with them. If there is a reason that isn't logistically feasible, for example, if the parent wants to go to the bathroom, it is helpful if there is a contained place they can go.

Many families are able to have the child's bedroom be a place they can go if they need to be separated from other household members when there is not adequate supervision. A door alarm can be put on the child's door and set overnight so that if they leave the room when others are sleeping, the adults can be alerted, and everyone can be kept safe.

I used to work with a family that decided that rather than get an alarm, they would lock the child into his room every evening and let him out again in the morning. Do not do that. Your home is not a prison; it is not safe or appropriate to lock someone in overnight. The locked-up child would have less chance of surviving if there was a fire or other emergency. The alarm lets everyone stay safely supervised without putting anyone's life in danger.

TL;DR

- People are often surprised to realize that they have been able to adjust to their "new normal," and managing the day-to-day tasks of living does become possible.

- It is important to think through the logistics of appointments and activists and to try to work with professionals who are geographically convenient when possible.

- The importance of adults listening to and taking seriously the thoughts and feelings of the hurt person cannot be overstated.

- Safety must continue to be the top priority, even as things start to feel more settled and manageable.

Key Terms in This Chapter:

Aftercare: Continued out-patient treatment following completion of residential treatment. (National Institute on Drug Abuse (NIDA), "Principles of Drug Addiction Treatment," 2018)

Chaperone: A person responsible for monitoring interactions to ensure safety. (Association for the Treatment and Prevention of Sexual Abuse (ATSA), "Practice Guidelines for the Assessment, Treatment, and Management of Male Adult Sexual Abusers," 2014)

Protective parent: A parent who takes appropriate action to protect their child from harm. (American Professional Society on the Abuse of Children (APSAC), "Guidelines for Psychosocial Evaluation of Suspected Sexual Abuse in Young Children," 2017)

Residential treatment: Intensive treatment program where the client lives at the facility. (American Academy of Child and Adolescent Psychiatry (AACAP), "Principles of Care for Treatment of Children and Adolescents with Mental Illnesses in Residential Treatment Centers," 2010)

Safety plan: Document required for special events outlining behavioral guidelines and boundaries. (Mentioned in the Community Rules section, derived from Beacon treatment manual by Dr. Nicolas Carrasco)

Safety rules: Specific guidelines put in place to prevent further abuse and protect vulnerable individuals. (Center for Sex Offender Management, "Comprehensive Approach to Sex Offender Management," 2008)

Chapter 7

Engage – Engaging with Treatment and Court

Navigating the criminal justice system in the United States, whether juvenile or adult, is daunting. It can be very helpful to have a lawyer involved whose job is to advocate for you or your child. Lawyers who are familiar with this type of law, as well as the judges, other attorneys, and norms of the area in which you live, can help advise you on what options are available and what might be the best course of action. Some families opt not to involve a lawyer, which is your choice for the most part. Either way, make sure you understand what is happening with legal procedures, how information gathered in any assessments might be used, and what options exist.

Finding a lawyer can be both expensive and daunting. If you cannot afford a lawyer, one may be available to you through the public defender's office or perhaps through a local non-profit legal organization. Like therapists, lawyers specialize, and it is important to make sure you are working with someone familiar with the law and issues around sexually based crimes. While it is possible to represent yourself, the complexity of the law may make that difficult and put you at a disadvantage if the case is settled by plea agreement or goes to trial.

If you are assigned a public defender or are qualified for some other type of legal aid, you may not get any choice about who your lawyer is. Of course, if you are paying privately for a lawyer, then that will be a lawyer of your choice.

There are many questions that are important to ask a potential lawyer, including but not limited to:

1. How long have you been practicing?

2. Have you handled many cases involving sexual crimes?

3. Have you handled cases in the adult or juvenile court?

4. How many of your cases have gone to trial?

5. What are the likely outcomes/reasonable expectations for a case like mine?

6. What kinds of things will be important to the judge?

7. How much and what kind of communication should I expect from you?

8. What are your fees, and what is the payment structure?

9. How much do you expect this will cost in total?

10. Should the person being prosecuted start therapy prior to court happening?

11. Are there any assessments or evaluations that need to be done, and should I find someone to do those or get those done through you?

12. Are there expenses that may come up that I should be prepared for?

13. Who will be working on my case?

14. What else should I know that I didn't think to ask about?

In almost all cases, only the defendant (the person accused of committing the crime) will need a lawyer. That being said, I once worked with a family who lived in a county where the district attorney at the time was very aggressive with the victim. The victim was told that if she chose not to testify against her abuser, they would ask the judge to detain her.

I would hope it goes without saying that it is never okay to threaten someone who has been the victim of a crime with legal consequences for having been hurt, but in this case, that is what happened. The non-offending parent of this victim decided that given the level of hostility directed at her, it would be best for her to have her own representation, and they hired a lawyer to help ensure that her rights were being upheld and that no one would be able to bully her into doing things she was uncomfortable doing.

Many cases involving illegal sexual behavior are handled in the courts by the defendant agreeing to a plea deal. It is essential that everyone understands what is being agreed to. I have often had discussions with individuals on probation who are surprised to learn about some of their requirements and conditions as they either were not told by their lawyers the details of what they were agreeing to or were perhaps too overwhelmed at the time to ask questions and/or remember the answers.

That can be especially disconcerting when the client is unaware of or has forgotten about something that significantly impacts them. For example, I once worked with a man who served a lengthy prison sentence. When he was released, he was under the impression that he had completed all the legal consequences of the crime he had committed. After a few months, he was informed that when he was originally sentenced, the prosecutor separated one of the charges, and the judge sentenced him to a separate and additional sentence of ten years of probation to be served after his release.

That meant he had to participate in and pay for treatment, follow probation rules, meet with his probation officer regularly, and continue to pay court and probation fees, all things he had not thought applied to him. Due to some circumstances particular to his case, the court also decided to place him on a GPS ankle monitor, the monitoring of which was also something he needed to pay for. It was overwhelming for him and difficult to adjust to.

Unsurprisingly, the first year or so of his probation and treatment didn't go particularly well for him, partly because he was so angry about the situation. Knowing all the details about what is going on in your own case is important and can help avoid having unanticipated problems later.

For the person who was hurt, it is usually also essential to understand all the aspects of what is going on in court. It is common for the person who caused harm to take a plea agreement. When that happens, it ensures that the person who got hurt does not have to testify in court, which can be very stressful, especially for a young child.

If the person does have to testify, it can be useful to spend some time with the prosecuting attorney who can explain what to expect and also help ensure you know what resources are available to you to make testifying less overwhelming. Some areas have therapy dogs that can accompany children into court; and in some areas, depending on the age of the person involved and the details of the case, a child may be able to testify away from the actual courtroom so they don't have to see everyone and can be seen through closed-circuit television.

In addition, there is an organization called Bikers Against Child Abuse (BACA), who gather to support children and help them feel safe. A few of the children I have worked with who have been victims of abuse have worked with BACA. While I have not personally worked directly with them, I have only heard wonderful things about them and their ability to support children in scary situations.

Talking to a therapist can be scary, even if you have decided on your own to make an appointment and you were the one who chose the person you are going to work with. Most folks who are court-ordered to treatment don't get a lot of choice about who they see, which makes feeling comfortable in therapy an even bigger challenge.

When I first meet with court-ordered clients, they often believe that I am out to get them, or that my goal is to catch them doing something so that I can recommend they be locked up, or that I do this job because I secretly hate them and want to punish them. None of those things are true.

It can take a while for people to feel calm enough to be open to the possibility that I wouldn't be working in this field if I didn't want to help folks and my goal is that they have the safe, healthy, and happy life they want for themselves. That is true of most mental health professionals. As a whole, we aren't out to get you.

That being said, we know that people have better outcomes in therapy if they have a good therapeutic relationship with their provider. Not every therapist is a good fit for every client. If you find that you have difficulty establishing a good relationship with a therapist that you, or your child, has been court-ordered to see, it is probably a good idea to discuss that with the therapist, the probation officer, or the judge.

If you live in a more populated area, it is likely that there are other therapists in the area who are qualified to help you, and you may be able to transfer to one of them. If you live in a more rural area, that may be more problematic. If, for logistical or legal reasons, it is necessary for you to work with a provider you don't feel comfortable with, please reach out to that person to discuss it.

I have worked with clients who have been uncomfortable or angry about something I said or did or an assumption they have about what I might be thinking. When the client is willing to talk to me about it, we have always been able to solve the problem. When I have had clients unwilling to talk to me about it, it becomes much more difficult, as I am not good at reading minds, and we can't fix what we can't discuss.

For pretty much all clients, both court-ordered and voluntary, letting their therapist know that they are uncomfortable with something the therapist is doing feels very vulnerable and scary, but it is also the only way to solve the problem.

As I said earlier, I often talk to court-ordered clients who were not aware of or prepared for some of the requirements of the plea they agreed to or the sentence they received in court. One of the things I often hear is a misunderstanding of what is meant by "treatment." Often, adult offenders will tell me that their lawyers have told them that therapy isn't a big deal, that they will just have to show up and pay, and everything will be fine. They are then surprised to find that sex-offense-specific treatment has a lot of requirements, can be very difficult, and is often emotionally painful. What is required in treatment varies from provider to provider and is often specific to the individual client, but it helps to know in general what is often expected.

For adults, sex offense-specific therapy generally requires that the client attend one group a week and individual sessions at least once per month. The length and intensity of treatment depend a lot on the requirements of the jurisdiction you are in and the client's level of participation and progress. I have had treatment programs in areas where adults on probation were required to be in treatment for the length of their probation, sometimes with the added requirement that if they did not make significant progress or complete treatment by the end of their probation term, their probation would be extended until they did.

I have also worked in areas where the length of time in treatment was solely determined by the client's progress, and I was able to graduate clients from treatment before the end of the term of their probation. It is important to read the terms of your probation paperwork carefully and to talk to your probation officer so you know what is likely to be expected of you.

Most providers use a treatment manual. This helps ensure that all the topics necessary are covered and gives the client, provider, probation officer, and judge a way to measure progress, as completing and getting assignments approved is a measurable way to show you are doing what you are supposed to be doing.

It is important to remember that the manual is a tool in treatment, not treatment itself. Some clients will need additional work on things that are not in whatever treatment manual they are using, and some clients might not need every chapter or may need the assignments modified.

It is also important to remember that simply completing all the assignments does not mean someone is successful in treatment. If you complete the whole workbook but don't change your behavior, then you have not yet been successful in treatment.

Similarly, for juveniles, most treatment programs are a combination of group and individual sessions. Prior to 2020, I generally expected the juveniles I worked with to attend group once per week and individual sessions at least twice per month. In addition, parents were asked to attend parent groups once per month, and depending on the specific needs of the individuals involved, family therapy sessions happened as well.

The COVID-19 crisis, of course, meant that there were no in-person sessions and no group sessions at all for a while. Many providers have returned to pre-COVID groups, but some have remained working primarily in individual session-only formats. We know from research and clinical experience that a combination of group and individual sessions is often the best methodology for this type of treatment, but it is not always logistically possible to do that.

Almost every juvenile I have ever worked with, and most adults, too, have told me they did not want to be in a group. They all explained to me how group probably wouldn't work for them and that they would be a better fit for individual sessions only. As an introvert myself, I understand the reluctance. However, for most, the group ends up being a very valuable part of their experience.

Nearly all the court-ordered clients I saw in 2020, both adult and juvenile, expressed to me their surprise about how much they missed the group once we had to stop having them. All the clients who started after 2020 and then had to adjust to us restarting groups, which we did in 2023, initially told me they were going to hate it and later let me know they were really glad we had group. After a client attends their first group session, I always ask them how they felt about it, and inevitably they say, "That wasn't as bad as I thought it would be."

Engaging with treatment providers and all the other professionals who end up being involved in sex offense cases can be daunting. Depending on the specifics of your situation, there are often a lot of us involved, and usually, you don't have a choice about who everyone is and what role they are filling. It is important that you understand who everyone is and what role they are there for.

It is also important, particularly for the person who caused harm, that you understand what the expectations are for you, as there may be legal consequences for not doing what is expected. If you are confused about an expectation, make sure you ask for clarification. If there is something that you know will make things more difficult for you, for example, not having reliable transportation, please be sure to let the professionals know so that they can be aware and perhaps help you find solutions.

There are people who are not good at their jobs in every profession, and that is true in the legal and mental health worlds as well. In the over twenty years I have worked in this field, the vast majority of professionals that I have met or worked with have been ethical, responsible, and dedicated to helping the people that they work with.

TL;DR

- It is often useful to hire an attorney who is familiar with this area of the law and can advocate for you and advise you about what is likely to happen.

- Establishing a good therapeutic relationship with your treatment providers is a significant factor in success.

- Even if you do not have a choice about who your therapist is, it is a good idea to talk to them about things that make you uncomfortable, even when that is scary.

Key Terms in This Chapter:

Court-ordered treatment: Mandatory therapy or counseling required by legal authority. (Legal/Clinical composite definition)

GPS ankle monitor: Electronic device used to track an individual's location as part of legal supervision (Department of Justice definition)

Plea deal: A legal agreement between defendant and prosecutor to resolve a case without trial. (Legal definition, Black's Law Dictionary)

Therapeutic relationship: The working alliance between therapist and client that facilitates healing and change. (APA Dictionary of Psychology)

Treatment manual: Structured guide for therapeutic intervention containing specific assignments and measures of progress that provide a framework for treatment delivery. (Clinical practice definition)

Chapter 8

Treatment – What to Expect from Therapy

The journey toward healing begins with a single step—finding the right therapist—yet this crucial first move often feels like navigating a complex maze. Whether you're seeking help voluntarily or through a court order, the process of connecting with the right provider involves more than just checking boxes for location, schedule, and insurance coverage. It's about finding someone who has the expertise you need and creates a space where healing can begin.

Think of finding a therapist as similar to finding a specialist for a medical condition but with an added layer of complexity. While medical specialists are clearly labeled—cardiologists for heart issues, orthopedists for bone problems—mental health expertise isn't always as clearly marked. This search becomes even more nuanced when looking for someone with specific experience in sexual behavior problems, where both expertise and the right therapeutic approach are essential for success.

As I mentioned earlier in the book, some states have a specialized license for people who work with sexual behavior problems. If you live in a state that has that, it can make it a little easier to find an appropriate provider. Even in states that do not, there are often professional organizations, like the state chapters of the Association for the Treatment and Prevention of Sexual Abuse (ATSA), that usually maintain a list of members.

Those lists can be a helpful place to start. Of course, clients who are court-ordered are often assigned to a specific provider, so finding a provider on their own is usually not necessary.

A lot of families want to be in touch with a treatment provider prior to the court order for therapy. They are often looking for therapists with knowledge about working with someone with sexual behavior problems, even when seeking out a therapist for the non-offending family member, so it is useful to have an idea of how to contact a qualified provider.

ℬℭ

Therapy for the Person Who Caused Harm

Probably the most frequent reason I get contacted by people who have discovered sexual abuse happening in their household is confusion about what to do and fear that there is no help for the person who has caused harm. The good news is that treatment is available, and good quality treatment is almost always effective. Treatment can't work alone, though. The client needs to be willing to do treatment work and make safe, healthy choices.

When I was in graduate school, there were no classes on working with court-ordered clients, and the message I got from my professors was that for therapy to work, the client must have chosen, of their own volition, to participate. I have found that that is not necessarily true. While it is certainly helpful if the court-ordered individual agrees that he or she needs help and is committed to treatment from the beginning, often, that is not how people start.

Clients will have to "buy in" eventually, but I have worked with lots of folks who started out with hostility or insistence that they did not need or want therapy or that they would be able to successfully manage themselves through their own willpower, religious beliefs, or participation in a twelve-step program, who ended up doing well in treatment and were able to be successful.

Unfortunately, I have also worked with folks who are either unwilling to be safe in the community or are so afraid of their own thoughts and feelings they remain committed to not engaging in therapy. In some cases, particularly for youth, a higher level of care than out-patient therapy is necessary to get them back on track, and sometimes, though luckily, very rarely, they remain a threat to community safety, and a judge needs to decide how to move forward with them.

Therapy can be scary, but I have never worked with a client or family who regretted buying in and participating. I have worked with clients and families who let me know that they regret not engaging or not engaging sooner.

The specifics of what type of treatment any individual with sexual behavior problems will get depend on a variety of factors. One of the biggest factors is age. The type of treatment I engage in with a 10-year-old client is different than what I do with a sixteen-year-old client or forty-year-old client.

We use the term "sex offenders" or "persons with sexual behavior problems" to describe anyone who has been convicted of a sex crime or who has engaged in inappropriate or illegal sexual behavior. Those are very broad terms, as illegal and inappropriate sexual behaviors fall under a large and varied spectrum of behaviors.

There are differences when working with someone who has molested a friend or relative, someone who has sexually harmed a stranger, someone who has exposed themselves or recorded others without their knowledge, someone who viewed, sold, or produced illegal sexual material, and someone who used sexual behavior as part of other violent crimes.

The specifics of treatment for an individual are, in part, determined by the specifics of what they have done. Even with a treatment manual and a relatively standardized program, the specifics are adjusted to the individual needs of the particular client.

For the most part, outpatient treatment for clients with sexual behavior problems involves a combination of group and individual therapy. There can be reasons why therapy is conducted primarily in individual sessions, not groups.

For example, while I often treat young children with sexual behavior problems, I usually only have one or two at a time in my practice, so not enough to form a group. Similarly, I have in the past had treatment groups for adolescent girls, but usually, I only have one or two girls in my practice at any given moment, or I have girls who are of significantly different ages and wouldn't be appropriate to be in a group together.

There have been times in the past when I have seen girls in both group and individual sessions, and there may be a time when that will happen again, but currently, I see the girls that I work with in individual sessions only. Other factors determine if a particular client is a good fit for a group, but when possible, a combination of group and individual sessions appears to be the most effective approach.

Different treatment programs expect different levels of participation from non-offending family members. Generally, if the client is an adult, they can choose—or not—to have their loved ones have some involvement in their treatment. Many programs ask that adult clients choose a support person who is involved and can support them in making good choices. I have, however, worked with adults who did not have anyone in their lives who was appropriate for that role.

When the client is a child or an adolescent, it is commonly expected that the parents or guardians will have some level of involvement. In inpatient settings, there may be rules about how much and what kind of contact with parents is allowed, some of which may depend on the client's progress in treatment.

In outpatient settings, it is not unusual for a parent group to meet once a month. In addition, parents and guardians are usually expected to participate in chaperone training to support their child in following their rules and, depending on the family's specific needs, to participate in family therapy.

The field of treatment for people with sexual behavior problems is relatively new, and while we now have good research to inform us, the field has made a lot of mistakes along the way. It is very possible, likely even, that as more research is done, some of what I write about in this book will end up being obsolete over time. That is why it is important for providers in the field to attend conferences and keep up with the latest research.

In the beginning, the first treatment programs and approaches tended to be very shame-based, following a "break them down before you build them back up" approach. There was the underlying idea that in order for treatment to be effective, it was important to make sure clients felt as terrible as possible about themselves and were convinced that they were dangerous and needed to stay away from others, particularly children or anyone who might be vulnerable, for the rest of their lives.

It should come as a surprise to no one that being told you are a terrible person does not inspire clients to be honest about their thoughts and feelings and to feel safe to talk about things they were already deeply ashamed about. Research and common sense have made it clear that people are not helped by being berated.

Luckily, treatment approaches have evolved over time, and it is rare to find a provider now who believes that shaming people is useful. If you do somehow end up with a treatment provider who is unwilling to treat clients and families with dignity and respect, I would encourage you to talk with your probation officer, lawyer, or judge and find out if there are any alternative providers in your area that you could transfer to.

No matter what brings them to therapy, everyone should be treated with dignity and respect. As I said earlier, some clients come into treatment with hostility and anger, and they often are scared and ashamed. Treating them with dignity and respect can help them feel less defensive and also remind them of their own humanity. This is true of both the individual client and their family members.

The scope of what constitutes treatment will vary from program to program. Some of that is due to logistics. Often, residential treatment programs have more time constraints than outpatient programs and are, therefore, narrower in scope. Sometimes, the scope of treatment is largely determined by the court order. For example, I have worked with clients who had in their court order to work on specifics about domestic violence or chemical-dependency issues, in addition to sexual-behavior-problem-specific therapy.

The scope of treatment is also dependent on the needs of the individual client. Some clients need more extensive trauma work than others, some need more time to focus on their relationships with family members and others, and some have addiction issues that need to be addressed.

The number of factors that can impact the scope of treatment is vast, and the above is not by any means a comprehensive list; it is just some examples of what factors the treatment provider is likely to take into account.

Treatment programs often consist of a variety of psychoeducation, cognitive behavior therapy, and psychodynamic approaches. There are several models, like the good life model, on which many workbooks are based. Most programs use a treatment manual or workbook, and several good ones are on the market.

The workbooks themselves are not treatment; they are guides and treatment tools, and they need to be used in the context of a treatment program with input from the treatment provider. Years ago, I became aware of a secure facility for adolescents that handed out workbooks to the clients, told them to fill them out, and collected them back later with no input or discussion. That is not treatment.

The reason I am aware of that program is that I had an adult client who was court-ordered there as an adolescent. He got out and re-offended as an adult and ended up being ordered to out-patient treatment. There is no way to know for sure, but re-offense for adolescents who have good quality treatment is very rare, and I am pretty sure that if he had better quality treatment, he either would not have re-offended or his treatment providers would have known him well enough to know that he was likely to be a threat and handled his case differently.

Whatever the specifics of the treatment program, it is important that providers get to know their clients well and that clients feel heard and supported. Treatment is not an easy task; we are routinely asking people to talk about thoughts, feelings, and experiences that they never thought they would share with anyone and that they have a lot of shame about. Often, there are aspects of treatment that are painful for the client, and it is important that they feel safe to express themselves.

ℰ🙰ℭ

Therapy for the Person Who Was Harmed

In some ways, treatment for the person who was harmed is more straightforward than treatment for the person who caused harm. For one thing, many more therapists work with survivors of abuse than there are therapists who work with perpetrators of abuse, so it can be easier to find a provider. It is also easier to change providers if the one you initially choose is not a good fit, as there are usually no court orders or requirements for the person who was harmed to work with a specific provider. As mentioned earlier in the book, if reunification is a goal for the future, it is important to find a provider willing to participate in that process.

The type of therapy that is most effective will vary from person to person and depend on a lot of different factors. Just like for the person who caused harm, one of the more important factors is the age of the person. For a child, it is important to find a provider who has experience working with children and has an office that reflects that. I see people of all ages. While my office is appropriate for adults, it also has a section full of toys and equipment for play therapy when I work with children. The type of therapy must fit both the chronological and developmental age of the client.

While treatment for people who have been hurt has been around longer than treatment for people who have caused harm, it is still a field that grows and changes based on leaps in knowledge from research and our increasing understanding of how the brain processes trauma.

There are several good treatment modalities for trauma, and I encourage you to research them and reach out to providers who have credentials in the modalities you think will be a good fit for you. Some of those techniques include Eye Movement Desensitization and Reprocessing (EMDR)—one of my personal favorites—somatic experiencing, hypnotherapy, sand tray work (another favorite of mine), art therapy, Theraplay, and Internal Family Systems (IFS).

There are many good books about trauma treatment and about each of those techniques and others. This is not meant to be a comprehensive review by any means.

We also know that no matter the technique or approach, the most important factor determining whether someone gets help from therapy is the strength of the therapeutic relationship. I think it is important to "therapist shop" and keep in mind that if the first person you meet is not a good fit, that just means you need to keep looking; it does not mean that therapy is not for you. It is also important to keep in mind that peoples' needs to grow and change. I have worked with clients who have had excellent and useful therapeutic experiences with other providers but had gotten to a point in their work where they required something different and needed to change to a different therapist. If you work with a therapist who tells you that they are the only person who can help you, that is a good sign that you probably need to move on to someone else.

ॐ

Therapy for Parents and Other Family Members

Years ago, one of my colleagues was working with a teenager who was really struggling, and this was not a child who had a sexual behavior problem but a kid who struggled with crippling anxiety, depression, and some suicidal thoughts and behavior. The teenager was making progress in therapy, but it was a struggle for them.

My colleague recommended that one of the parents start seeing me, as that parent and child often ended up in conflict.

Once the parent started doing their own work, most of which had very little to do with the details of their relationship with their child and more to do with how the parent managed their own emotions, everything in the household started to relax.

The other parent also found a therapist, and the original teenager is now absolutely thriving in college. All the members of the household feel more settled, happier, and relaxed.

The progress the child made in therapy increased exponentially once the parents started their own therapy. This is not an isolated example; it can be expensive and logistically difficult for all household members to have their own therapist, and it can also be transformative for everyone.

It is also important to keep in mind the needs of any other children in the household. When sexual abuse occurs, the focus is usually on making sure that both the perpetrator and the victim receive the help they need. In many families, there are other siblings who were neither abused nor abusive. Parents often hope that their other children were spared the stress and trauma of the situation and were, therefore, mostly not impacted. It is important to keep in mind that family stress impacts all the family members.

In the aftermath of the discovery of sexual abuse, there may be changes to family structure and income, new household rules, and parents whose time and attention may be focused on other things, not to mention the general stress and tension. Even children who are not directly involved in what happened are likely to need support and therapy, and it is important that they do not get lost in the shuffle. Younger siblings are often not told exactly what happened, and in their confusion they may believe things that aren't accurate or decide that they are somehow the

101

cause of any stress in the family. It is important that, in an age-appropriate way, they are made aware of what is going on and reassured that they are not responsible for anyone else's feelings and that their own thoughts, feelings, and needs are important.

Often, in their rush to find help for their children and to deal with all the obligations that come with having a child on probation, and sometimes having children who have to live in different locations, parents forget to keep in mind the importance of their own well-being. Abuse and trauma are often multigenerational, and it isn't unusual for parents and other family members to have experienced things in their own lives that impact their well-being as well.

Even if an individual parent doesn't have their own history of abuse, parenting children who are struggling is very difficult and can be overwhelming. Often when I work with families, parents will assure me that they will be fine as long as their children are getting what they need. I can understand that sentiment. However, I have seen the tremendous difference it can make for the individual family members and the family as a whole when parents also engage in their own therapy.

I usually recommend to parents and other family members that they seek treatment providers outside the ones involved in the adolescent treatment program. The reason is that if you, as a not-court-ordered client, go to therapy with a typical provider, you have the high level of confidentiality that any client going to therapy has.

There are times when, for logistical or other reasons, a family member of a client who is in our program will end up being a client of one of the therapists who is not directly involved in the treatment of the individual who is court-ordered. That can be very helpful in terms of communication and the professionals' ability to share information with each other. However, if that is the case, it is important that everyone understands what can and might be communicated to whom.

For example, I have sometimes been the therapist for the victim of someone who was seeing another therapist in my office for the crime. That is very helpful when coordinating reunification and also having a greater understanding of the whole picture of how the family functions. When that situation occurs, the client needs to know that while I am not the offender's therapist, I still go to the probation staffing meetings where we discuss all the clients in our program, and information I know from my work may be part of those discussions.

TL;DR

> • Treatment can be a lot of work and is often emotionally painful, but it is a necessary part of moving forward.
>
> • Finding a treatment provider that is a good fit may take some time and effort.
>
> • Even though it can be logistically difficult, it is very helpful if every member of the household has their own treatment provider.

Key Terms in This Chapter:

Chaperone training: Specialized training for approved adults who supervise offenders in community settings. "Community Supervision Protocols," (Center for Sex Offender Management, 2021)

EMDR (Eye Movement Desensitization and Reprocessing): Trauma therapy technique using bilateral stimulation to process difficult memories. (EMDR International Association)

Good Lives Model: Strengths-based rehabilitation framework focusing on building capabilities for a fulfilling life. (Ward & Brown, 2004)

Internal Family Systems (IFS): Therapeutic paradigm that views every human as a system of protective and wounded inner parts led by a core self. (IFS Institute)

Outpatient treatment: Therapeutic services provided while the client lives at home. (Healthcare definition)

Probation staffing meetings: Regular meetings of the multidisciplinary team, including probation officers, treatment providers, and other professionals collaborating to monitor and support the progress of the client in court-ordered treatment and their families. (*Treatment for Youth with Sexual Behavior Problems*, Duncan, 2023)

Psychoeducation: Educational intervention providing information about mental health conditions and treatment. (*APA Dictionary of Psychology*)

Sand tray therapy: Expressive therapy technique using miniatures and sand for nonverbal processing. (Association for Play Therapy)

Somatic experiencing: Body-focused trauma therapy approach addressing physical and emotional trauma symptoms. (Somatic Experiencing International)

Theraplay: Attachment-based therapeutic approach focusing on parent-child relationships. (The Theraplay Institute)

Chapter 9

Yourself – Don't Forget Self-Care

When your child is in distress, everything else in life becomes background noise. Yet paradoxically, your ability to function well—especially during a crisis—directly impacts your child's well-being. Like the airline safety instruction to put on your own oxygen mask before helping others, parents must learn to maintain their own emotional balance while supporting their children through trauma. It may not feel intuitive to focus on your own well-being when your children are in distress, but without some balance, it will be nearly impossible for your family to thrive.

American culture generally tends to celebrate people who can push through and "deal" with situations. We brag to each other about how little sleep we get and how much caffeine (and other substances) we need to function on any given day. There is a reason why cultures that emphasize pushing through, working endless hours, and being productive at all costs are also cultures that have high rates of preventable disease, autoimmune disorders, and mental health struggles. Unfortunately, for many people, it takes a crisis, perhaps a health crisis or maybe a personal one, for them to step back, re-evaluate, and make some changes in support of their own well-being.

There are many good things about living in a society that values independence and personal achievement. However, the dark side of that emphasis is that it can sometimes be at the cost of a sense of community and connection with others. Humans are social creatures, and even those of us who don't particularly like socializing need to connect with others to function well.

A lot of people already feel a sense of isolation and disconnection from the surrounding community; loneliness is something of an epidemic at the moment. Dealing with the aftermath of sexual abuse can make that an even greater problem. People rarely feel comfortable letting friends, family, or acquaintances know what is happening, and even if they do, often other people have no idea how to respond.

As a society, we generally don't talk about sexual things, let alone when sexual things go wrong. Having sexual abuse happen in the family can feel very isolating, and at the very time one could benefit from support to help cope with an overwhelming situation, people are the least likely to reach out to their community.

Communities also don't necessarily know how to respond if someone does reach out and lets them know what is going on. I have worked with many clients who were in treatment for having committed a sex offense and who had been involved in religious communities and found that their community had no idea what to do when they were honest about it and asked for support.

Sometimes, organizations are able to navigate that information successfully, but many of these clients were required to leave their communities or were treated in ways that made them want to leave.

On the other hand, years ago, I worked with an adult offender who was very open with the people around him. When he and his wife purchased a home in a new area, they had a neighborhood barbeque, and he let all his neighbors know about his history. He explained to everyone his safety rules, his work in treatment, and what his wife's role as his chaperone was. In his case, his neighbors appreciated his honesty, and his whole community became a tight-knit source of support for him.

This person was on the sex offender registry, and by introducing himself and explaining himself honestly, he avoided the response people often have when they search the registry and find that they have someone in their area who is a registered sex offender. Ironically, had that client asked my opinion prior to the neighborhood BBQ he and his family hosted, I probably would have cautioned against it. Happily, it ended up working out well, and the neighbors were not only a support to him but also to his wife and children, who got great benefits from the sense of community that developed.

As mentioned earlier in the book, most treatment programs for adolescents have some kind of parent group that meets once a month or so. It can be extremely helpful to get to know others who are experiencing some of the same things you are experiencing. It helps to see that the other families are regular people, just like you, and that having had sexual abuse happen in your family doesn't mean that you are somehow broken beyond repair.

This happens in families across all races, ethnicities, religions, socio-economic statuses, and education levels. Some treatment programs for adults also have a support group available for the partners or family members of the adult offender. However, that is not as common as it is for adolescent treatment programs. It is, though, helpful to be reminded that you are not alone.

For parents, that may mean carving out time to hang out with friends, going to a movie, reading a book, exercising, or doing whatever else it is that helps them feel relaxed and fully themselves. For many parents, it is important that they get additional care both for themselves as individuals and often for their relationship. This can be logistically challenging.

Years ago, I worked with a family whose oldest child abused their middle child. The authorities chose not to prosecute the case, so the family had no legal obligation to pursue treatment. It was important to them that their children and family be healthy, so they chose to seek out treatment anyway. The oldest child saw a colleague of mine to address the sexual behavior problem; the middle child saw another colleague to help them cope with what had happened to them; the parents saw me occasionally to consult about the process and ensure they were doing everything they could to support their children's well-being.

As time went on, they realized that their youngest was also overwhelmed by all the changes and tension in the family, and that child began seeing a therapist as well. The parents ended up having some struggles in their marriage, in part related to all the stress, and they addressed that with a marriage counselor. All told, these folks had a whole team of mental health professionals that they worked with to help put things back together again.

The last time I heard from them, things were going well. The oldest child had done well in treatment and was making safe choices in their daily life; the middle child had processed their trauma and now focused mainly on typical middle-school social dynamics; and the youngest one continued to feel supported and safe. The parents stayed married and were able to work through the stresses that had happened.

It was not an easy or short process, and while they had financial resources and good insurance, it was also not cheap. There were times when the stress felt overwhelming for everyone involved, but they were brave and determined and were able to move toward healing.

As adults, it is usually our job to put the well-being of our children first. After all, children don't have the resources—financially, emotionally, or intellectually—to handle situations on their own. In addition to making sure you balance that with some care for yourself, it is also important to evaluate if the way you are trying to support your child is having a negative impact on both you and the child. Some types of "support" can cause harm to everyone involved.

The vast majority of adolescents I have worked with have been able to remain in the community and live safely with their families. Occasionally, that is not the case. I can remember a young man who had abused his younger siblings. He was required to have no contact with them and so lived with his grandparents, who loved him very much. Unfortunately, this young man struggled a lot with needing to control everyone around him, and he chose to do that through attempts at manipulation and fear. His grandparents very much wanted to support him and did not want him to need to go to a residential setting. However, he frequently engaged in behavior that made them very uncomfortable and was sometimes threatening. The impact of that much stress began to affect the grandmother's health, and over her objections, it became apparent that he needed a higher level of care.

He was ordered to a residential treatment facility where he would be able to get the more intense treatment he required, and his grandparents were able to live without having to be on guard all the time in their home. Moving him to a higher level of treatment not only supported the well-being of the adults in his life but also supported his well-being, as outpatient treatment wasn't giving him what he needed at that point in his life.

His grandparents' desire to protect him from what they viewed as a harsher punishment made sense, but it ended up being a situation where they put themselves in danger and kept him from getting the help he needed, which was only available at a higher level of care setting.

In the case above, the grandparents were initially reluctant to let the treatment providers know what was going on at home for fear of getting him in trouble. Once the information came out, the treatment team was able to work toward getting everyone what they needed. It was not necessary, nor useful, for the grandparents to sacrifice their safety in their attempt to support their grandson. Often, parents or guardians will be guarded or secretive about some of the child's behavior in the hopes of helping the child avoid getting into further trouble. While I understand the impulse, I have only ever seen it backfire and negatively impact both the child and adults. Treatment providers can't help with problems that we don't know exist, and it isn't unusual for small problems to grow when ignored.

There is a 5.6 trillion dollar global wellness industry, and yet rates of depression, anxiety, and other mental-health-related struggles seem to always be on the rise. Doctors frequently advise their patients to manage their stress in order to help with a wide array of both physical and mental health issues. Despite all the advice and resources, it can be surprisingly difficult to identify all the sources of stress in one's life and figure out how to manage them effectively.

Many people bristle when told to "slow down and breathe" during moments of distress. While breath management is indeed a powerful therapeutic tool, such advice often comes across as dismissive.

Stress management is easier when it makes sense, so it helps when one understands how stress impacts the body and what mechanisms help us maintain a good balance.

It seems odd to say that it can be difficult to notice stress and understand its source because, for the most part, we feel like we can tell when we are stressed or not. It is important to remember that there is more than one way to experience stress; it is not always emotional in nature, and we don't always notice the impact until it has grown to significant proportions.

Have you ever been driving somewhere, noticed that your hands hurt, and then realized you have a death grip on the steering wheel, even though nothing scary is happening on the drive? Or have you suddenly become aware that you are clenching your fist or have your shoulders shrugged up by your ears, and you don't know why? It is not unusual for our bodies to react to perceived stress without us even noticing. It is important to remember that humans naturally strive for homeostasis—our body's tendency to maintain stability. While

111

scientists now prefer the more precise term "allostasis" to describe this self-regulating process, we'll use "homeostasis" throughout this book for simplicity. For a more in-depth discussion, check out books about neurology, nervous system response, or anatomy and physiology.

The impact of our system working to achieve homeostasis means, basically, that we adjust to incremental stress in a way that sometimes makes it hard to recognize and also hard to deal with. The process is complicated and typically involves many systems functioning throughout our bodies that we have no conscious control over and often no awareness of. So, it isn't surprising that we are usually mostly unaware of what is happening until we reach a crisis point.

Our bodies and brains are so committed to homeostasis that we will quite often find it easier to stay in a situation or state of mind that is painful than it is to change, even when the change is beneficial.

People generally think of relaxing as something that is pleasant and feels good. While that is usually true in the long run, it is very important that people realize that when working on relaxing and managing stress, it is often fairly unpleasant at first. I don't think that is something that most people are aware of, so when they try to relax and find it irritating or unpleasant, they believe they must be doing it wrong and give up. Please keep in mind that, for the most part, our brains and nervous systems hate change, so even positive change comes with challenges.

I was born with a rare genetic bone disorder. For me, it was a spontaneous gene mutation; in other words, no one else in my family has it despite it being genetic. Since it is rare and usually runs in families, I didn't get an accurate diagnosis until I was in my mid-forties, which means for the majority of my life, I had no idea I had a chronic pain condition. It may seem odd to say that I didn't realize I had chronic pain. You would think I would have noticed, but that is an example of how easy it is for people to normalize things and how difficult it can be to understand our own experiences as we don't have an outside frame of reference.

As you might imagine, being in pain without acknowledging it led to both a lot of tension in the way I carry myself physically and the way my nervous system reacts to things. I was pretty much unaware of that for most of my life, as it just felt normal to me. I started working with a vestibular physical therapist over a year ago to try and manage some of the impact, and even though I know better, I was and often continue to be shocked by how unpleasant learning to relax physically has been.

The net benefit is definitely worth the effort, but the process is not always as pleasant as one would think relaxing should be. My nervous system has spent my whole life trying to find a way to protect me from unacknowledged pain, and getting it to calm down about that is a slow and challenging process.

So, if you find stress management difficult and frustrating, be aware that you are normal. That is just how our brains and nervous systems work. Give yourself some grace.

So what is stress exactly? In his book, *Why Zebras Don't Get Ulcers*, Robert Sapolsky describes a stressor as anything in the outside world that knocks you out of homeostatic balance, and the stress response is what your body does to reestablish homeostasis. That is a very broad category of things and includes things that we don't always think of as stressful. For example, I have noticed that weather can be a significant stressor both for myself and, once I started tracking it, for many of my clients. In the past, thinking of the temperature and barometric pressure as a source of stress hadn't occurred to me, and now that I notice it, I am often surprised at how big an impact it can have.

The list of things that can be or are stressors is vast. Stressors can be categorized in various ways, and the following is a list of categories that I think can be useful.

1. Physical stress – over exercise/exertion or not enough exercise/exertion, over or under the physiological needs of food, water, sleep, oxygen/breathing

2. Cognitive stress – too much or too little brain activity, resulting in fatigue and inability to sleep well

3. Emotional stress – life events that result in uncomfortable or overwhelming feelings

4. Chemical stress – external or internal, can come from food, medication, irritants, addictive substances, etc.

5. Environmental stress – heat, wind, cold, barometric pressure, dryness/humidity, air quality

6. Social stress – isolation, bullying, loss of a loved one

7. Relationship stress – finances, arguments, or breakups, communication difficulties, etc.

8. Professional/educational stress – conflict at work, job loss, grades, exams, etc.

As you can see, some of the categories overlap, and some events would create stress in several categories simultaneously. Discovering that sexual abuse has happened in your household is a stressor that could potentially impact nearly every one of the above categories. It would be difficult to overstate how overwhelming it is to deal with the aftermath of abuse for everyone involved.

Stress management does not mean trying to have a life with no stress in it; not only would that not be possible, but it wouldn't even be healthy. Our systems are designed to handle the ups and downs of stress in our lives, and the key is not "no stress" but a healthy balance in the ways our system responds to stress. There are often things we can do to minimize or eliminate certain sources of stress. For example, leaving an abusive relationship. But some sources of stress are outside our control. In addition, some sources of stress are not things we want to eliminate. For example, athletes and performers feel stressed prior to a game or a concert, and also performing or playing is something they generally look forward to and enjoy and not something they would want to give up. The benefits outweigh the stress, and in fact, for many people, the rush of adrenaline in competition or during a performance is part of what draws them to their sport or art. It can be helpful to understand how stressors impact us and then work toward managing stress in a way that minimizes the negative impact it can have on well-being. Easier said than done.

Stress, tension, and our body's response to them are universal human experiences, and yet, in many ways, oddly we know little about how our systems work. As technology and research have improved, we have rapidly been learning a great deal more about how our brains function and the interaction of our nervous systems with all the rest of our bodily functions. We have a long way to go, and I suspect in the next few decades, our knowledge base will increase significantly, but even with the knowledge base we currently have, we know significantly more about how the stress response works than we did even ten or twenty years ago. The following is a very brief, definitely not comprehensive, description of how our bodies handle stress. Several good books on the market explain the biology and neuroscience more in-depth if you are interested in a more detailed and complete overview.

There are a few ways that people divide the brain when talking about what parts do what. In his book *Just Listen*, Mark Goulston talks about the brain having three layers: the lizard brain, the mammal brain, and the human brain. In the book *The Whole Brain Child*, the authors, Daniel Siegel and Tina Payne Bryson, talk about the upstairs brain and the downstairs brain. When talking to clients, I often refer to reactions coming from the back of the brain versus the frontal lobes of the brain.

Whatever descriptor or metaphor resonates with you, it basically comes down to the information that some of our brain operates and makes decisions almost completely based on sensations and feelings, and some of our brain works on thoughts and higher-order abstract thinking. Unfortunately for us, those parts of the brain don't usually talk to each other much, so we often react in ways that make sense to our brain but don't necessarily reflect the information we might know.

For example, many people are terrified of spiders, and they may logically know that the spider in their house is teeny compared to them and that it is very likely to be harmless and easily dealt with and also that having spiders around can be helpful in terms of managing other pests. None of that information helps when you are afraid of spiders, though, and the fear reaction just happens; logic doesn't get in the way.

That can be extremely frustrating for people with an irrational fear of something; knowing it is irrational does not do a lot to help make the fear less.

We have a built-in protection system in our brain that is focused on trying to ensure survival. It is important to note that the system is there for survival, not happiness or joy. There is a part of our brain called the amygdala. This is the part that is always scanning our environment for danger. Once it notices something that it has decided is a threat, it immediately responds with what we often refer to as the fight/flight/freeze response. This system works faster than thought, which is often a good thing. If a speeding car is heading for you as you cross the street, you don't want to spend any time thinking the situation through, calculating your speed relative to the car, thinking about the angles of approach, and assessing the odds of an impact. No matter how fast you can do math in your head, you would have already been flattened by the time you do all that. What you want to have happen is that you jump out of the way and then after, think, "Wow, that car was coming fast."

The difficulty arises because the amygdala isn't a particularly good judge of what is life-threatening and what isn't, and once it decides something is dangerous, it can be very difficult to convince it otherwise. By the time you can use your logic and knowledge, from the frontal lobes of your brain, you have already reacted to the perceived threat, sometimes in ways that are not at all helpful. It would be very useful if our brains could do a better job of distinguishing the difference between things that are actually life-threatening and things that are uncomfortable, but for the most part, we can't, not without a lot of work anyway.

Most people are aware that going up on a stage to perform or give a speech or presentation at work or in school might end up being uncomfortable or embarrassing, but it is very unlikely to be life-threatening. Nonetheless, lots of people suffer from debilitating stage fright, and their brains and bodies act as if speaking in front of others is as dangerous as entering an enclosure full of lions. Trying to calm themselves down through logic alone is rarely useful.

The stress/anxiety reaction comes from the nervous system, which pays almost no attention to logic and is mostly impacted by body responses, which is why breathing and muscle relaxation are frequently the most effective means of interrupting those kinds of stress responses.

In addition to generating a survival response to things that aren't particularly threatening, another interesting quirk of humans is our ability to stress ourselves out through our thoughts alone. We often worry about things long before they happen, sometimes things that are very unlikely to actually happen. Unfortunately for us, our brains react the same way to a situation we experience in person and a situation we are just thinking about.

Other animals have a similar stress response as humans, but as far as I know, we are the only species that responds to imagined future stress.

The amygdala can learn from experience. For example, my youngest child played club volleyball for many years, which means I attended an endless number of volleyball tournaments in large convention centers with hundreds of teams all playing at the same time and volleyballs regularly flying everywhere. At the first major tournament we attended, I got hit in the head by a ball coming from a different court.

Interestingly, I believe that was the last time I was hit, though we attended what felt like hundreds of tournaments over many years after that first one. After that first hit, my sensory system adjusted to be on the lookout for volleyballs, even when I wasn't. I noticed I could duck out of the way of oncoming balls, even if I had been looking at something on my phone, was talking to another parent, or watching my daughter play. My sensory system adjusted to being at a tournament and kept watch despite my not consciously being aware. It only took being hit once at the first tournament for my brain to figure it out. That was super helpful and, I imagine, saved me from many head injuries and concussions.

My same sensory system, however, has also decided that if I turn my head and look to my right, I am in danger. When I look to my right, my heart rate elevates, I get dizzy, I often get a headache, sometimes a rush of heat, and occasionally I even have difficulty breathing. There is absolutely nothing dangerous about looking to my right, but when I do it, all the blood in my system rushes to protect my vital internal organs, and I am left with odd, annoying symptoms.

I do not know why my nervous system decided looking to the right was dangerous. I suspect my amygdala formed a connection at some point when I was a kid between looking to the right and a day or time I had a pain flare, but I don't really know. It is such an odd symptom that it took me a while to figure out. Once I became aware that it was a trigger, I could start working on desensitizing it and helping my brain accept the idea that looking to the right isn't dangerous.

Changing the nervous system can be a slow process. After about a year of becoming aware of the issue, I can now usually look to my right successfully, often for minutes at a time, without triggering a stress response. Sometimes, the things our amygdalas decide we need protecting from make total sense and are easy to identify, like flying volleyballs, and sometimes they don't. The intellectual knowledge that looking to my right is not dangerous has no impact on my nervous system response.

Our brains are optimal at responding to life-endangering threats that resolve fairly quickly. For example, being chased by a lion. In the past, it would have been very useful for our sensory system to notice the signs that a lion was nearby and then decide to hunt it, run from it, or hide from it. Once the danger had passed, our systems could return to normal function, so the time we were engaged in the stress response (increased heart rate, a flood of stress hormones, lack of digestion, etc.) was relatively brief, and then we returned to a sense of safety, which would have been the norm.

In our modern society, most of the threats we face are not life-threatening in nature and are not as clearly resolvable as dealing with a lion, where we either survive or don't. Most of the stressors we face today are social, emotional, or societal, not fatal, but since our nervous systems can't distinguish between what is life-threatening and what is just annoying or uncomfortable, it is not unusual for people's brains and bodies to be in a near-constant state of alarm.

Since our systems crave homeostasis, the state of alarm, of flight/fight/freeze, can end up feeling like the norm, and a sense of safety ends up feeling unusual, uncomfortable, or strange.

Living in a constant state of stress response has a lot of unwanted impacts. A constant flood of stress hormones has a significant negative impact on both mental and physical well-being, and research has shown us that there is a significant connection between people who have experienced a great deal of stress and trauma and many chronic and some acute health issues. Modern medicine often likes to pretend that physical health and mental health are two separate things, but the truth of the matter is that each individual is one whole being. What impacts mental health also impacts physical health and vice versa.

In modern Western society, we are generally socialized to place more importance on intellectual function than any other way of understanding the world. In fact, we often pride ourselves on our ability to "push through" and ignore the messages we get from our nervous system.

In my own journey to understand and manage my nervous system response, I have realized that my nervous system has been trying to get my attention since I was a very young child. I just never knew how to listen to it or how to interpret the way it communicates. Life would be much easier to navigate if our nervous systems communicated with words, but they do not. I believe that understanding how the nervous system works and interacts with the rest of our body is a good first step in figuring out how to deal with its impact.

Without getting too complicated or technical, there are basically two parts of the autonomic nervous system that are important for this discussion. The sympathetic nervous system (SNS) is the part that gets activated when we have a stress response, and the parasympathetic nervous system (PNS), sometimes called the "rest and digest" part, is the part of our system that returns us to calm after a stressor. Both the SNS and the PNS are connected throughout our bodies, but the SNS has many more connections than the PNS, which contributes to the difficulty of calming our systems down once activated. Making it even more difficult, the SNS also reacts much faster than the PNS does, so not only does the PNS touch fewer internal functions than the SNS does, but it is slower to impact those systems. If calming down feels hard, that is because it is.

The autonomic nervous system controls the things that our bodies do automatically, like breathing, heart rate, temperature regulation, etc. Often, changes happen in those automatic processes without us really being aware of them. It can help to know what systems are impacted when our brains perceive a threat and the SNS is triggered. When the SNS perceives that we are in a situation that poses a threat, our eyes dilate, our heart rate increases, muscles in the airway relax to improve oxygen intake, sweat production can increase, production and release of glucose increases so there is a burst of energy available, digestion slows to allow energy to be used for other things, etc. When people experience SNS response, and there is not a life-threatening situation to respond to, they can experience digestive issues, dizziness, fainting, the inability of the heart rate to respond to exercise, rapid heart rate, sweating too much or not enough, and vision problems, among other symptoms.

Knowing how the stress response works can feel a little overwhelming. After all, it seems pretty clear that we are wired in a way that contributes to it being much easier to be in a state of stress than a state of relaxation. It seems weird to have to work at relaxation, but once you get into the habit and learn how to hack your system, it is very doable. One of the first steps I recommend to clients is to check in on what is happening physically. Many people have thyroid disorders; the thyroid controls a great deal, including, for many people, depression. If you have an untreated thyroid disorder, appropriate medication is likely the only thing that will help. Therapy alone won't make much of a dent. Similarly, many people have untreated sleep apnea and other sleep disorders. If you are usually tired, even if you get enough sleep, or if you suffer from insomnia or other difficulty sleeping, it would be a good idea to talk to your doctor about getting a sleep study done. All the therapy in the world won't compensate for not getting enough oxygen to your brain overnight. So, first things first, if you have the financial ability, get a good physical and request testing if your doctor doesn't suggest it.

While you are addressing what might be contributing physically, it is also a good idea to start practicing activating your parasympathetic nervous system. While it can be slow to activate, the good news is that there are many ways to activate it, and most of those are pretty straightforward, if not as automatic as the things that activate the sympathetic nervous system. Some are things you can do on your own for free, and some are things you might need to reach out to a professional for. A basic start for managing your nervous system is the underlying things humans need to function well: sleep, hydration, nutrition, and movement. If you have too little or too much of any of those four things, it is likely that you will be struggling. In addition to those four things, the following is a list, not at all comprehensive, of things that can help activate the parasympathetic nervous system.

1. **Breathing** – in particular, diaphragmatic breathing, in other words, breathing in a way that fills your diaphragm. The easiest way to do this is to put the tip of your tongue behind your top teeth, inhale through your nose and

allow your abdomen to expand, then exhale through your mouth. You may want to move the tip of your tongue to go behind your bottom teeth when exhaling and allow your abdomen to contract again. Try to exhale for a little longer than you inhale. This will signal to your nervous system that things are okay and that it is safe for the parasympathetic nervous system to come online and help calm you down.

2. **Muscle relaxation** – this works well on its own but is particularly effective in conjunction with the breathing described above. Often, our muscles are tense in ways we don't even realize. Wiggle your fingers and then wiggle your toes. It's often helpful to shake your arms some to relax the arm and shoulder muscles. Starting at the top of your head and moving down, scan your body and consciously relax each part of you until you feel looser and heavier. You may notice feeling more connected to the ground you are standing on or whatever surface you are sitting or lying on. It can help to think of yourself as melting into the surface that you are on.

3. **Meditation** – there is a lot of information available about meditation in books, online, and in apps, so I'm not going to go into a lot of detail here. One thing that I think is important to note, however, is that meditation is not the achievement of cognitive calm but the practice of directing your attention. Many times, people tell me they are not good at meditating because they get distracted by their own thoughts and their minds wander. That is normal and expected; the benefit comes from noticing the distraction and gently redirecting yourself back to your breath, using the guided meditation you are

listening to, or whatever focus you have chosen. If you practice meditation frequently, it is likely you will eventually be distracted less often, but it is not likely you will get to a point where your mind never wanders off. That is fine, and it is the practice of deliberately directing your attention that is the useful part.

4. **Prayer** – for many people, reaching toward the divine, however they define it and in whatever way works for them, can have a similar impact as meditation. Many religious practices include praying in community, which can be beneficial on many levels. Many people, however, have also suffered from pain related to religion, and if this is something that is painful or doesn't resonate with you, then move on to other things.

5. **Acupuncture/Acupressure/Cupping** – Chinese medicine has a different, though complimentary, lens than Western medicine typically does. The practices of acupuncture, acupressure, and cupping come from the perspective of how the nervous system and the different parts of the body interact with each other. These approaches can be very helpful in the quest to help regulate and balance nervous system response.

6. **Exercise** – particularly types that focus on stretching, breathing, and balance. I think one of the reasons that exercises like yoga, tai chi, and qigong are so popular is that focusing on breathing, stretching, and balance stimulates parts of our brains that help with regulation throughout many of our body's systems. These are good ways to convince our brains and nervous systems that there is no danger and that it is safe to relax.

125

7. **Walking** – walking is another form of gentle exercise that can be immensely beneficial. Research has shown significant benefits from walking across pretty much all body systems, and if you walk outside, you can often add the benefits that come from being in nature at the same time.

8. **Nature** – research shows that spending time in nature can help calm and regulate human systems.

9. **Massage** – this is another activity that has research-based benefits for helping to calm and regulate the nervous system and allow restorative rest.

10. **Bath/Shower** – most people find a hot bath or shower relaxing and helpful. Ironically, cold showers or ice baths are good for interrupting anxiety responses, though people typically find them unpleasant.

11. **Music** – most of my clients report that listening to music is one of the most consistent coping strategies they use to deal with stress. Many people create playlists they find helpful for different moods and different circumstances. Learning to play an instrument or sing, and in particular doing that in a group like a choir, also has research-based benefits for overall well-being.

12. **Playing with Pets** – Interacting with animals can be relaxing and very beneficial. There have been studies that show that petting a dog or cat can lower people's blood pressure.

13. **Grounding** – grounding is the practice of connecting with either the ground or the surface you are sitting or lying on. You can place your feet on the floor and focus on feeling connected to the surface you are on. The

metaphor of melting into that surface is often helpful. Grounding is a practice that can be done almost anywhere and under nearly any circumstances; combined with breathing and muscle relaxation, it is a reliable way to bring your parasympathetic nervous system online.

14. **Engaging in an enjoyable activity/hobby** – engaging in an activity you enjoy, which can allow you to focus on something that is not stressful or overwhelming, can be very helpful. These activities can be almost anything and often can be done solo or in groups. Some examples include creating art, knitting/crocheting, making music, dancing, putting together a jigsaw puzzle, engaging in sport, participating in electronic or tabletop games, and putting together Lego or model kits.

15. **Ice Packs/Cold Shower/Plunging Face in Ice Water** – plunging into cold water is not exactly relaxing. However, as mentioned, it can be an excellent way to interrupt anxiety or panic. It is kind of like a built-in reset button in humans. Cold water triggers a body response that activates the parasympathetic nervous system. Dunking your face in ice water is typically not only effective but also works quickly. Cold showers and ice packs can also be useful. I keep an ice pack in my office freezer to give to clients who need help interrupting panic or anxiety attacks when they are in my office.

Overall, while it is easier to get stressed than it is to calm back down, it is worth the effort to consciously choose to engage in activities and think in ways that help activate the parasympathetic nervous system and allow your brain and your body systems to rest, relax, and restore. Because you are reading this book, it is likely you are currently involved in one of the more stressful experiences of your life. Make the effort to give your systems a break so that you can be the person and the parent you wish to be.

TL;DR

- It can be difficult to find community when dealing with sexual abuse in your home, but it is important to remember you are not alone.

- Stress management and relaxation are not always as intuitive as people think they might be, and learning about how your body and brain react to things can be helpful.

- There are a lot of paths to help your nervous system relax, so find the ones that work for you and practice them regularly.

Key Terms in This Chapter:

Allostasis: Process of maintaining stability through physiological or behavioral change. (McEwen, *Hormones and Behavior Journal*, "The Concept of Allostasis in Biology and Biomedicine," 2003)

Amygdala: Brain structure responsible for detecting and responding to threats. (AbuHasan Q, Reddy V, Siddiqui W. (2023). Neuroanatomy, Amygdala. StatPearls Publishing; https://www.ncbi.nlm.nih.gov/books/NBK537102/)

Diaphragmatic breathing: Deep breathing technique engaging the diaphragm muscle. (Hamasaki H. (2020). Effects of

Diaphragmatic Breathing on Health: A Narrative Review. Medicines (Basel, Switzerland), 7(10), 65. https://doi.org/ 10.3390/medicines7100065)

Fight/flight/freeze response: Automatic physiological reaction to perceived harmful events or threats. (*Harvard Review of Psychiatry*, "Fear and the Defense Cascade")

Grounding: Therapeutic technique connecting one physically or mentally to the present moment. (van der Kolk, *The Body Keeps the Score*)

Homeostasis: The body's tendency to maintain internal stability and balance. (Cannon, *The Wisdom of the Body*)

Nervous system regulation: Process of managing and balancing autonomic nervous system responses. (Porges, *The Polyvagal Theory*)

Parasympathetic nervous system (PNS): Part of the autonomic nervous system responsible for "rest and digest" functions. (Tortora & Derrickson, *Principles of Anatomy and Physiology*)

Stress response: The body's reaction to any change requiring adjustment or adaptation. (Sapolsky, *Why Zebras Don't Get Ulcers*)

Sympathetic nervous system (SNS): Part of the autonomic nervous system that activates the "fight or flight" response. (Marieb, E. N., & Hoehn, K. (2022). *Human anatomy and physiology* (12th global ed.). Pearson.)

Chapter 10

Fear – Dealing with Worries About the Future

Parenting is hard and often full of worries under the best of circumstances. Parents worry if they are making the right choices from the very beginning, everything from what to eat or drink while pregnant, choices about feeding, using a pacifier, how to handle sleeping and toilet training, to decisions around schools, discipline, and extracurricular activities. It is likely that you have worried about some of these choices, and it is even more likely that people have given you their opinions about what you should or shouldn't do, even if you didn't ask for them.

When sexual abuse comes into the picture, the more typical worries about parenting can shift, and worries often become more overwhelming and intense. You may still get unsolicited advice from others, though more often, you may find that people don't know what to say and sometimes even turn away from you and your family. How to handle sexual abuse, both when someone has been victimized and especially when someone has hurt someone else, is not a topic most people know much about. Unfortunately, there are a lot of myths and false information out there that can make a scary situation feel even scarier.

When families first come to my office after the discovery of sexual abuse, everyone involved is worried. Parents worry about the well-being of their kids; they worry that they did something to cause this or that people will think badly of them. They worry about the future, that they won't make the right decisions now, and that they and their children will have even bigger problems in the future. If two parents are involved, they worry that they might not agree on the path forward and that they may have a future of strife and stress with their partner.

Those who have caused harm often carry multiple worries: concern for their victims' well-being, fear that they are irreparably broken and that everyone hates them, anxiety about legal consequences, and guilt about damaging their family relationships.

Meanwhile, those who were hurt struggle with their own set of fears: wondering if they'll get in trouble, feeling responsible for the consequences to the person who hurt them, believing they've caused family turmoil by speaking up, questioning if they'll ever feel safe or trust others again, and worrying about their path forward.

Many of these fears can be addressed as the legal system sorts itself out and the people involved start to get the help they need. Don't be surprised, however, if some of these fears take a long time to fade and if some come back from time to time.

Recently, I was talking with a client of mine who was abused by her father many years ago. She has done remarkably well in therapy and is a healthy, thriving adolescent with the same concerns as any other child about to start high school. On this particular day, however, she had been thinking more about what had happened to her than usual, and she wondered during her session if she would be able to have a healthy relationship with a future partner or spouse or if she would end up choosing problematic or abusive partners in the future. She wondered if she would ever feel comfortable with the idea of dating and the possibility of having sex with someone in the future.

This is not a fear that is present for her all, or even most, of the time, but it surfaces occasionally. Healing isn't linear, and even when things feel significantly better almost all the time, it isn't unusual or a sign that progress in therapy has been reversed to sometimes revisit things that had felt resolved before.

While each family's situation is unique, certain fears and questions surface repeatedly in my practice. Here are the most common concerns families raise during our first conversations.

What did I do as a parent to cause this, and how can I prevent it in the future?

Many factors go into someone reaching the point where they are willing to hurt another person in that way. While it is possible that parenting can contribute to that, I know lots of kids who have engaged in inappropriate and illegal sexual behavior and ended up going down that path for reasons unrelated to their relationship with their parents. It is not likely that you are a direct cause of the abuse; humans are too complicated for that, and also, parents don't control their children's behavior. There are things you can and should do to help minimize the future risk of sexual behavior problems. However, the only person who can choose to be safe or not is the person who caused harm. It is difficult to stop someone determined to do something because you cannot control anyone but yourself. It is, however, important to put things in place to make it easier to make safe and healthy choices and to address any issues that might have been contributing factors to the abuse.

Most families I have worked with are careful to help support their children in being safe. However, I have worked with court-ordered adolescents whose parents insist on taking them to high-risk places without adequate supervision, and even some parents who have told their child that they need to babysit for younger family members. As I said before, you cannot control other people, and a person who is determined to do something is difficult to stop. However, it is not okay to put people in a situation where they are likely to fail. Very few adolescents re-offend, but few is not zero. The children I know who have re-offended have almost always been in situations where others encouraged or demanded that they not follow their rules.

Will my child, who got abused, ever be the same again? Are they broken now?

Our life experiences, combined with our individual genetic tendencies and the broader culture we are in, shape who we are. That being said, people who have survived sexual abuse are not broken or damaged or whatever other negative message they tell themselves or perhaps heard from others. Humans are, interestingly, both rather fragile and remarkably resilient in the face of adverse circumstances. For some people who have experienced sexual abuse, that abuse becomes a rather defining experience that they struggle with across their lifespans. For some people, it becomes a bad thing that happened to them in the past but not necessarily something that impacts them in their day-to-day life. So, what is the difference between those two categories, and how do you help someone move from the first category to the second? While the severity of the abuse involved often plays a role, what seems to be the most impactful factor is how people react when the abuse becomes known.

Some of the clients I have worked with who have had the biggest struggles are people whose adults or community, upon finding out about the abuse, either ignored it, encouraged it, or blamed the victimized person for what happened. I have worked with many people whose moms were angry with them for "seducing" their fathers, stepfathers, or other men in their mom's life. I have also worked with many people whose parents told them they were imagining or exaggerating and that nothing was happening.

I don't think I'll forget the young lady I worked with whose mother had given her twenty dollars a week to stay quiet about what her stepfather was doing to her. Those kinds of reactions set up a situation that contributes to a long-term struggle for the person who was hurt.

If that happened to you or someone you know, don't panic; hope isn't lost. There are still many paths to healing and resilience, and it may just be more work and time than it would have been if the reaction from people around you had been more helpful.

In contrast to abuse survivors who are ignored or blamed, children and adults who have people around them who react in kind, protective, and supportive ways tend to experience an easier path to healing. It is important to ensure that the person who was abused is believed, supported, and allowed to have whatever emotional reaction they have at any point.

It is also important that the victimized person has a therapist who has experience working with survivors of sexual abuse and trauma to work with. Whenever possible, it is also important for the person who was hurt to feel in control and have some choices about how things are handled. One of the things abuse does is remove your sense of control over yourself and your body; returning to that felt sense of control is very helpful for people.

Will your child be exactly who they were before they were abused? No, of course not. Experiences change people, but they absolutely can be healthy, thriving individuals who have the kind of life they would like to have.

Will my child, who abused someone, ever be safe? Are they destined to be an adult offender? Can they get married and have kids?

One of the most persistent myths about people who commit sex crimes is that they are beyond help and are destined to be dangerous, scary individuals who need to stay away from children and other vulnerable populations for the rest of their lives. Most news media, TV shows, movies, and "common knowledge" support this myth. No matter how many TV cop shows you watch, it is still a myth and not based on reality. That is not to say that every individual who has committed a sex crime ends up being safe in the community; people have to choose to be safe, and some people choose not to be. That being said, the recidivism rate for sex offenders is actually much lower than most people think and is even lower for adolescents who commit sex crimes. Adolescents and adults who successfully complete a high-quality sexual behavior problem-specific treatment program are very likely to be able to be safe, healthy individuals who pose very little risk to the community.

Let me be clear: That does not mean that it is not important to be mindful of safety and have rules and boundaries in place. It is, in fact, very important. A low recidivism rate is not zero recidivism, and community safety should always be the top priority.

Did something happen to my child who abused someone that I don't know about? Are other people in my family being hurt or causing harm?

There are many reasons why someone engages in inappropriate or illegal sexual behavior. Sometimes, there is a history of that child having been abused in some way, not necessarily sexually, but also, sometimes, there isn't. Sometimes, families will report, or perhaps discover, that there has been abusive behavior going on among relatives for a long time throughout many generations, but also, sometimes, there hasn't been. It is important to realize that every situation is individualized and that figuring out the "why" of sexual abuse is often a process that takes time and needs to acknowledge many contributing factors.

I am so overwhelmed and angry all the time. Will I ever feel okay again?

This is an overwhelming situation, so if you sometimes, or even nearly always, feel overwhelmed, then congratulations, you are human. It would, in fact, be very strange if you sailed through the experience of dealing with sexual abuse in your family unbothered and always calm and relaxed. That said, it will get better. The beginning of adjusting to all the court-ordered requirements, or if the court was not involved, the process of finding the right resources for your family is overwhelming and stressful. Eventually, a new normal gets established, and doing what you must do to ensure safety will be second nature.

Changes in lifestyle and logistics can be significant. However, there are times when the adjustments are more subtle, but either way, you will get to a place where things start feeling more settled. For many people, that is helpful but not enough, and it is important that, as discussed in Chapter 9, you take care of yourself as well. Many parents feel that the most important thing is that their kids get help, which is certainly true, but the kids are also watching you. I can't begin to estimate how many kids I have met with, both survivors of abuse and perpetrators of abuse, who tell me how much they wish their parents would go to therapy as well. I have also seen families totally transformed countless times because one or both parents had the courage to reach out for help for themselves. I don't think it is possible to overestimate the impact that has.

Will I be able to forgive my child who abused someone?

This can be a difficult issue for people to address, as parents often struggle to balance the needs of all the children involved. Many parents have talked to me about loving and wanting to support their child who caused harm and also knowing that if it had been anyone else who had hurt their other child, they would likely want that person to be severely punished or hurt. It is important, particularly if you are having persistent negative feelings about your child, that you find a qualified therapist to process those feelings with. No child, even a child who has engaged in harmful behavior, deserves to be treated badly, nor can a child thrive in the face of persistent dislike from the adults around them.

I remember a conversation I once had with a mom about her son who had abused her daughter. We were preparing for reunification, and the mom told me that she "fucking hated him" and that also she could cover that up and that she spent time with him and supported him. I do believe she thought that was true. However, hiding your feelings from your kids is a difficult thing to do. The little sister told me on more than one occasion that she needed to handle some things regarding her reunification with her brother with just my support, as her mom was not yet "over it" and would not be able to handle it. Similarly, while nervous about his sister's well-being during reunification, the young man was more worried about his mother's ability to manage herself. As much as she thought she hid it, he was well aware of how she felt. Luckily, she was willing to eventually start working with a qualified trauma therapist and was able to have a supportive environment with that therapist that allowed her to start working through her own feelings and reactions. Her willingness to get help for herself has contributed to her family being on a path toward healthy functioning.

Are other people going to find out? How do I face the rest of the family? What must the judge, probation officer, and therapist think of me?

In some cases, families do not have much control over who knows what happened and who doesn't. There are cases that end up in the news, or the offense occurs outside the home and is known by people in the community. Sometimes, someone involved tells someone they think they can trust, and that person unexpectedly tells others. However, the information can often remain private with the family and the various professionals involved.

Sometimes, the person who was hurt does not want many people to know, and in some cases, that person feels better when they let people know what happened to them and can tell their story to others. Whenever possible, the person or people who were victimized should have as much control as possible over who knows what happened to them.

It is also true that abuse within the family can cause ripple effects. I once worked with a teenager who had abused not only their sibling but also some cousins. This family had a family-run business, which complicated the situation. The parent who worked in the family business ended up deciding to move on to another job to decrease the stress and tension in her relationship with her family members, many of whom were making different choices about how to handle what had happened than she was. If I remember correctly, the family eventually reconciled, but the stress was significant for all involved.

On the other hand, I have also worked with clients whose extended family has been an invaluable source of support and help. In general, truth is easier, and often, hiding things from close family members is difficult and adds to the overall stress level.

Many of my clients worry a lot about what I and the other professionals involved think of them. Please keep in mind that while this is likely one of the most overwhelming and embarrassing things you have dealt with in your life, for those of us who work in this field, it's just another day at work. I have worked with hundreds of families who have family members who struggle with their sexual behavior, and I can guarantee that there is very little that I find surprising, shocking, or bothersome. That is true of all the professionals I work with. The worry about being judged can contribute to some folks not being totally honest with the professionals they are working with; please keep in mind we are here to help, and we can't help if we don't know what is going on. I know my mind-reading skills are terrible, and I can say with confidence that this is true of everyone who works in this field.

What will happen if my ex finds out? Will they use this to try to take custody of my kids away from me?

This is usually a question for your lawyer. If you have been involved in a high-conflict custody battle, having someone in your home who engages in problematic sexual behavior might be something that your ex-partner would want to bring up in court.

Personally, I have only seen significant changes in custody agreements happen when it is logistically necessary to separate some of the children. For example, I used to work with a young man who abused his younger sister. He and his sister lived with his mom and visited his father and stepmother every other weekend. His stepmother also had children; they lived primarily with their father and visited their mom and stepdad every other weekend. Prior to the abuse, the families had it set up so all the children would be visiting the father and stepmom on the same weekend. After the abuse came to light, the biological father of the other two children was uncomfortable with that, and the family started staggering the visits so the son was not at the house the same weekend as the stepsiblings. In that case, the amount of time the children spent with each parent didn't change, but the amount of time they spent with each other did.

On the other hand, I have also worked with kids who were abused by a stepparent or partner of their parent, and the parent refused to separate from the abusive adult or be protective of their child. In those cases, that parent will likely lose custody of their child, as they are unwilling to help them stay safe.

Will my child who was hurt feel unsupported if I also help the child who caused harm? How can I help them both? Can my family ever be together again?

Supporting both children can be a difficult balance to find. If the children need to be separated, it should, whenever possible, be the child who caused harm who is inconvenienced. The person who was victimized should not have to move households, change schools, or avoid activities they want to participate in.

On the other hand, the child who caused harm is still a child and needs the love and support of their adults as much as any other child. If the child who caused harm has to live with other relatives for a while, it can be difficult for the parents to ensure they are still spending time with that child and staying involved in their life, especially if their move takes them far enough away to make spending time together difficult.

Every family has their own unique situation and will find its own path to supporting its children.

Often, the child who was harmed worries about and wants to see the child who caused harm, especially when siblings are involved. Usually, when I work with the younger sibling, I have found that while there may be a period in the beginning when they don't want to hear anything about the older sibling, that doesn't usually last very long, and they end up becoming concerned that by speaking out about what happened, their older sibling may be suffering.

It is important that the person who was victimized knows that speaking out about what happened to them was a good thing for everyone, so more often than not, knowing that their sibling is getting what they need makes everyone feel better, not unsupported.

I have worked with a few families where reunification was not in the best interest of the people involved, and the family was not reunited; however, that is unusual, and most of the time, families do well being reunited, particularly if both the victimized person and the person who offended are children. Whether your family can be together again is too individualized a question for me to answer in a book, but the likely answer is probably.

Will my child who got hurt start hurting other people when they get older?

There is a persistent and damaging myth that all people who have sexually abused others have been sexually abused

143

themselves. Some people have taken that myth and expanded it to create the additional and incorrect myth that people who have been sexually abused are likely to sexually abuse others when they get older. I have met with more than one adult client who was sexually abused as a child and who had a friend, family member, or even a doctor warn them that they should be careful about having children as they are now likely to cause children harm.

That is total and complete nonsense; anyone who tells you that has a very poor grasp on how humans and trauma work. Most people who get hurt do not go on to cause any harm to others. It is true that sometimes kids who are sexually abused act out that trauma with others, and that is one of the reasons why it is so important for kids to get the therapeutic help and support they need, but there is no reason for someone who was sexually abused to worry that they will grow up and hurt their future children.

As mentioned in other parts of the book, sometimes sexual abuse is a part of multigenerational trauma. It is something that happens within a family in every generation, which may be part of where this myth originated from, but that pattern has much more to do with individual specifics of how families with multigenerational trauma function than it does with sexual abuse somehow being like a vampire bite that turns whoever is bitten into an abuser.

ℰↃଓଌ

You likely have some fears that I did not address in this chapter. It is also likely that I didn't address the specifics of your situation. Fear can be overwhelming and make it difficult to function. Decisions made from a place of fear often don't have the most useful outcomes. It can be helpful to write down any questions or worries and bring that list to a meeting with the mental health professionals involved in your case. Usually, your fears, while individual, are not that different from ones others have, and a therapist who is experienced in working in this area should be able to help explain what is happening and what might happen and help you gauge how realistic your fears are.

I once worked with the father of a teenager in our treatment program who, because of things he had experienced in the past, was terrified that the courts would take his child away from him and that if his child did anything that wasn't exactly perfect, he would be put in prison never to be heard from again. This led to the parent not allowing the child to participate in nearly any social or extracurricular events, and the parent nearly made himself ill with worry if they got caught in traffic and were late for an appointment.

When I first met with that parent, he asked me the same few questions ten or fifteen times throughout the appointment because he was so scared he couldn't hear or process my answers. It took many conversations before he started to recognize that my colleagues and I were there to help him and his son and that we were not out to get him.

His fear was understandable; he had had some bad experiences in the past, but the intensity of it made both him and his child pretty miserable for a while. If you find yourself similarly worried, please reach out to the professionals involved. Most of the time, this isn't as scary as it seems it might be.

TL;DR

> - Parents often worry about the choices they make for their children. When sexual abuse happens, the worries can be bigger, and it may be difficult to find resources and advice.
>
> - Everyone involved is likely to have a long list of worries and fears.
>
> - While the things you are worried about may be particular to your situation, others likely have similar worries, and the professionals in your life will be able to help you sort through them.

Key Terms in This Chapter:

Multigenerational trauma: Trauma patterns passed down through family generations. (van der Kolk, *The Body Keeps the Score*)

Trauma response: Physical and emotional reactions to traumatic events. (International Society for Traumatic Stress Studies)

Chapter 11

Integration – Putting the Pieces Together

At the beginning of this journey, it may have seemed endless and daunting, but eventually, you likely adapted to the requirements of courts, probation, and treatment. Then, one day, you are almost done. The person who was hurt is no longer as focused on healing from what happened and has started spending more time and energy on other concerns. Perhaps clarification and reunification have happened, and everyone's living situation feels more stable. You are informed that the child who caused harm is nearly done with their treatment and will soon graduate and be successfully discharged from probation. It's a goal that has likely been at least a couple of years in the making.

The goal of putting this experience in the rearview mirror and moving forward may feel scarier than you thought it would. It is not unusual for my clients to start dragging their feet on things when they get toward the end of treatment; some of them even end up doing things that create some problems as a way to sabotage their progress.

While nearly everyone looks forward to no longer having to go to court, respond to probation officers, or be required to go to treatment, it is also likely that some of those things have become a big support over time, and the thought of losing the support can be overwhelming.

Every therapist is different, but I always like to make it clear to my clients that just because they are no longer court-ordered to see me doesn't mean that they can't make an appointment and see me anyway. Some clients do continue to schedule sessions, sometimes briefly and sometimes for a longer period, and some do not, but knowing they have the option can make transitioning away from the intensity of court-ordered treatment less daunting.

For the person who was victimized, the transition may be a little different, as there is not usually a hard line for them between being court-ordered and being released from probation requirements like there often is for the person who caused harm. Often, the kids I have worked with have expressed concern that their parents are bringing them solely for the purpose of clarification and reunification and that when that process is over, they won't be able to come back. It can be helpful for them to know that they can continue to have as many or as few appointments as they would like.

Often, one of the biggest adjustments for individuals and families when they start probation is the number of rules they must follow. People routinely have a long list of rules given to them by the court and probation. In addition to that, rules are often given to them by the treatment provider that are a requirement of being in treatment. Even for clients who are not court-ordered, there are usually rules from their treatment provider and often Child Protective Services. One of the tasks of transitioning off probation and required treatment is to decide what rules are important to maintain and what feels safe to let go of.

The specific rules any individual has been given will vary from jurisdiction to jurisdiction, depending on the specific treatment provider, and will likely be individualized to the specific person involved. The following is a baseline list of rules that I normally use with clients who have been court-ordered to see me because of a sexual behavior problem. They, of course, get modified to fit the individual circumstances of specific cases. These are taken, with permission, from the Beacon treatment manual, which was written by Dr. Nicolas Carrasco.

HOME RULES

1. Be fully dressed when not sleeping or in the shower.
2. Always wear underwear.
3. Knock on the bathroom or any closed door before entering.
4. Always lock the bathroom door when using the bathroom or showering.
5. Do not view R-rated or horror movies, especially movies that contain sexual violence and/or violence toward women and children.
6. Do not listen to music with sexually degrading lyrics.
7. Do not play video games rated "A" or "MA."
8. Do not view or possess pornography.
9. Do not have female peers visiting the home unless parents are home.
10. Do not be in any private place with a person you are sexually attracted to.

11. Sleep alone at all times.
12. Do not carry or sit children on your lap.
13. Do not have contact with children more than two years younger than you without your chaperone being present. (Contact means being in the same room, having a conversation, or exchanging letters, gifts, etc.)

COMMUNITY RULES

1. Be fully and appropriately dressed at all times - no sagging, no underwear showing.
2. Wear belts at all times unless wearing pants with an elastic waistband.
3. Do not go to places where children gather without adult supervision.
4. Keep my hands to myself at all times.
5. Do not go to teenage clubs without permission from the probation officer.
6. Do not touch or expose my private parts in public.
7. No sexual behavior in public, including kissing.
8. Do not view R-rated, extremely violent, or horror movies.
9. No sexually explicit language in public.
10. Do not make obscene or sexual gestures in public.
11. Prepare safety plans for all special events.
12. Do not stare at people for more than two seconds.

SCHOOL RULES

1. Keep my hands to myself at all times.
2. Do not stare at people for more than two seconds.
3. Do not be alone with people more than two years or younger than me.
4. Do not sag my pants or shorts.

5. When using the bathroom, use a stall.
6. Do not touch or expose my private parts at school.
7. Girlfriend/boyfriend should be at least fourteen years old and not be more than twelve months younger or older than me,
8. If my friends start making sexual comments, jokes, or gestures, leave. If I cannot leave, do not contribute to the conversation.
9. Do not use sexual language or make obscene gestures.
10. Do not touch other people without permission.
11. Do not possess or view pornography at school.
12. Do not sexually harass others.
13. Take pictures of peers only with permission and only of peers who are over eighteen years old.

GROUP RULES

1. Maintain confidentiality.
2. Be honest.
3. Bring a workbook, paper, and pen or pencil.
4. Be on time.
5. Do thirty minutes of work in your workbook per day.
6. Have an agenda to present.
7. Be respectful.
8. One person talks at a time.
9. Stay on topic and talk about treatment.
10. Give appropriate feedback and be helpful.
11. Do all special assignments.
12. Follow your probation rules regarding contact with the victim.

As you can see, there are some rules. For example, "Don't touch others without consent," which is important to be followed for the rest of someone's life. There are also other rules, like not watching horror movies, that likely can be safely let go of. It can be helpful to have a conversation with each other and your treatment provider to help ensure everyone is on the same page with what things will look like moving forward. It is particularly important if the person who was hurt and the person who caused harm are going to be seeing each other or living in the same household again that a conversation happens to ensure that the person who was harmed knows the plan and is comfortable with whatever decisions are made. That person's well-being and sense of safety should continue to have a significant impact on how decisions are made.

When families first start treatment, they are often overwhelmed and concerned that there is very little hope for the future. Hopefully, by now, that has changed for you; if not, please talk with the professionals involved. This isn't a quick or easy process, but it is very doable, and at the end of it, you are very likely to have established many healthy, low-risk lifestyle choices that will contribute to the kind of future you would like to have.

TL;DR

- Sometimes, moving on from probation, court requirements, and therapy is more stressful than anticipated.

- One of the tasks that can be helpful for the transition is figuring out what rules you want to keep in place and what rules can be relaxed.

- Getting through this process is not quick or easy, but it is doable.

Key Terms in This Chapter:

Treatment provider: Professional responsible for delivering therapeutic services and establishing treatment-specific rules. (Context derived from the chapter)

Chapter 12

Reunification – Should That Be a Goal, and How Does That Work?

Every family and individual impacted by sexual abuse is unique, and the goals that they have are not always the same. For some families, reunification is a goal; for some, it is not. Sometimes, it is a good idea and beneficial for all involved, and sometimes, even if it is a goal for some members of a family, it turns out not to be a good option. Some families never get separated, so reunification itself is not necessary, though clarification might be. If clarification and reunification are not in your future, feel free to skip this chapter.

Often, reunification, in one form or another, is a goal. In some situations, the person who was hurt wants to reunify in order to make sure the person who hurt them understands what they did, to ask why they did that, and to ask what that person is doing to ensure they never hurt anyone else again.

In some cases, the person who was hurt wants to reunify in order to have everyone attend large family gatherings without feeling uncomfortable, but outside of that, they do not have a lot of contact with the person who hurt them. There are also cases when the person who was hurt wishes to establish the type of relationship with the person who hurt them that allows them to see each other regularly while feeling safe and comfortable.

In other cases, usually when the person who was hurt is the younger sibling or other close family member of the person who hurt them, they want to go through the clarification and reunification process so that their older sibling can move back home and they can establish a healthy sibling relationship with each other.

Whatever the goal, the circumstances for your individual family are specific to your situation. In this chapter, I will discuss the basic process of clarification and reunification, what those things are, what they involve, and if that is a goal, how to go about getting there and how to know when it is the right option for everyone involved. Every jurisdiction and every provider will likely have a slightly different process, and the professionals in your area can advise you about how the process will likely work for you.

What does reunification involve, and is it the right choice? Reunification is the process that happens when the person who was hurt and the person who caused harm decide they want to be able to see each other again. This often, though not always, is the case when the two people involved are siblings or close family members.

The most important factor in any clarification or reunification process is the well-being of the person who was hurt. No matter how much any other member of the family, court officer, judge, or caseworker wants reunification to happen, it should never happen if it is not in the best interest of the person who was hurt.

The process of reunification can be complicated, but it usually starts with clarification. As part of sex-offense-specific therapy, most treatment programs require the clients to write something called a clarification letter. The court-ordered clients I work with are required to write this as a therapeutic exercise, regardless of whether they will actually be reunifying with the person they hurt.

This letter is written to make it very clear (that is why it is called "clarification") that the person who was hurt did nothing wrong and that all the responsibility for what happened is with the person who caused harm. In addition, it is important that the client makes clear that they understand the depth of the harm that they caused and that they let the person they hurt know that they have been working in therapy so that they learn how never to do that again and that they are open to answering any questions that person has.

This letter often does not contain an apology. That is because when someone apologizes, the other person can feel compelled to say, "That's okay" or something similar, and it is important that the person who was victimized does not feel compelled to respond in any way, especially in a way that would minimize how they feel. Later in the process, the person who caused harm can apologize if they wish, but the first step is to make sure that they take complete responsibility for their behavior and give the other person the space to respond in whatever way is helpful for them.

The clarification letter is a difficult letter for clients to write and is usually something they do after they have already been in treatment for quite some time. It often takes many revisions to ensure that the client is saying what they need to but also in an age-appropriate way that is not re-traumatizing for the person who was hurt.

No movement forward in the reunification process can happen until the person who offended is in a position to write this letter and be helpful to the person who was victimized in any possible future meetings. So, even though the victim's well-being is the most important factor, clarification will not begin until the court-ordered client has made enough progress in treatment.

Sometimes, that delay is difficult for the victimized person, who would rather reunify sooner, and some steps can be taken to relieve that person's distress, like notes exchanged through the therapists involved, which can help while they are waiting.

Clarification and reunification also should not begin if the person who was victimized does not have a therapist of their own. It is easy for parents and other family members, even when they do not mean to, to pressure someone to go along with reunification. It is critically important that the victimized person has a therapist they are comfortable with who can assess if reunification is what they truly want and is in their best interests and can advocate for them.

Ironically, the person who was hurt is often ready to participate in clarification and reunification before the person who caused harm is. If that is the case, and the person who was victimized has stopped having regular sessions with their therapist, they will likely need to reestablish that relationship for the reunification process. They can, of course, find another therapist if that is their preference.

It is useful if the therapist for the victimized person is supportive of reunification and has some familiarity with the process, though familiarity with the process is not a requirement. There are some agencies and individual therapists who are unwilling to participate in reunification at all. If at all possible, it is beneficial to have a conversation about that before the person who was hurt starts therapy and establishes a therapeutic relationship with a professional. It is not ideal for someone to have to change therapists in order to see their loved one again. I have seen that happen multiple times, and it is often a big loss and disappointment for the individual.

I will not go into much detail here about the content and process of writing a clarification letter. The specific requirements will vary from treatment program to treatment program. If you are interested in a more in-depth description, you can find it in my previous book, *Treatment for Youth with Sexual Behavior Problems*.

In general, as I said earlier, this is a place for the offender to be clear that they are totally responsible for what happened, that they understand how much pain they have caused, and that they are committed to never causing that kind of harm again and that they are open to answering any questions and doing what they need to do in order to ensure the safety and comfort of the person they hurt.

Once the clarification letter is written and approved by all the therapists involved, there are a few different ways to proceed, depending on the needs of the individual clients. In some cases, the person who was hurt would rather hear the letter for the first time directly from the person who hurt them, and sometimes, they prefer to preview the letter alone with their therapist so they can process their initial reaction privately with their therapist.

Often, when I am working with a child who has been hurt, we read that letter together in a session with the support person or people of their choice, usually a parent. If that is the case, it is important to meet separately with the parent first in order to ensure they know what to expect and to give them the space to process their feelings about what is happening so that they are less likely to get overwhelmed in the session.

It is important that the person who was hurt has all the time and space they need to process their reaction to what can be a very emotional experience without feeling like they need to take care of their parent. Most of the children I have worked with are distressed at the idea that their parent is distressed and will suppress their own reaction so as not to further upset an overwhelmed parent. If it is not possible for the child to not feel responsible for the parent's feelings, then it may be in their best interest to go over the letter alone with their therapist.

Once everyone is ready, there is usually a reunification session. If at all possible, this should occur in the office of the therapist who sees the victimized person. We want that person to feel as comfortable and at home as they can. That is not always logistically possible, but when it is, that is ideal.

The reunification meeting usually includes the offender and their therapist, the victim and their therapist, as well as whatever support person or people the victim would like to have in the room. These meetings are often very emotional, and as most of the kids I work with would say, "super awkward."

Hopefully, long before the meeting takes place, the person who was victimized has discussed with their therapist how they want the meeting to go. In my case, my office can get a little crowded when we have that many people in it, so we discuss if the client would still like to have everyone in that space or if they want to use one of the larger rooms in the suite that I have available.

We also discuss how they want to handle the reading of the letter and what, if anything, they would like to do in order to help with the awkward factor. We usually end up having snacks or pizza, board games, art materials, or anything else people can do with their hands. Sometimes, the initial meeting of everyone will just involve chatting and catching up on each other's lives. We save the heavier work of reviewing the clarification letter for a second session.

After the initial clarification meeting takes place, both the person who was hurt and the person who caused harm will need to meet with their therapists to discuss how they feel about how it went and what future plans are.

For some families, it is important to have multiple sessions with everyone attending. These subsequent sessions can involve reading the apology letter, discussing what rules need to be in place for the victimized person to feel safe, answering questions the child who got hurt may have, and talking about how the adults will handle situations if anyone gets uncomfortable.

These sessions can also involve playing games, doing art projects or sand trays, and generally just hanging out and getting to know each other again.

For some families, it becomes important to have sessions with fewer family members involved. For example, I once participated in the clarification and reunification between two siblings; after the first couple of meetings, the other therapist and I realized that both of our clients were working hard to manage the emotions of the adults involved. In this case the adults who had attended the initial meetings were the mom, the dad, and the dad's fiancée. The adults were not as good at managing the tension they had between them as they thought they would be, and it left the kids focusing on maintaining peace rather than their own feelings about the abuse that had happened.

In that case, we added some sessions that involved just the kids and the therapists, which helped the kids talk about what they needed to talk about and also helped us, the therapists, have a more accurate gauge of how they felt without the other family tension playing a role.

Some families only need the initial meeting with the therapists in the room, and they are able to quickly move on to beginning to see each other in public. Some families need many more subsequent meetings with professionals in the room. The deciding factor should always be the well-being of the person who was victimized.

Once the decision is made that the people involved can start to see each other on their own, it is still very important that it is a slow process and involves both the person who caused harm and the person who was hurt checking in with their therapists every step of the way. The initial visits should be relatively brief. For example, everyone gets together for a couple of hours for lunch or other similar activities.

Assuming those get-togethers cause no distress for anyone involved, the length of time can be gradually expanded. If the goal is for the people involved to live in the same house again, once everyone is comfortable being together for long stretches of time, an initial overnight visit can happen.

It is, of course, impossible for the person who caused harm to be supervised during a twenty-four-hour period, as people need to sleep. Before an overnight visit is scheduled, measures should be put into place to ensure safety and comfort overnight. Often, this means putting an alarm on the door of the person who caused harm so that if they leave their room overnight, the adults at home are awakened by a loud alarm and can come check to see what is going on.

In the past, I have worked with families who intended to lock their child into their room overnight in order to ensure safety. That is not a good idea. Locking someone in their room puts them at significant risk should there be a fire or other emergency.

The alarm allows parents to ensure they know if the child leaves their room without putting anyone in danger. Sometimes, the person who was hurt also feels more comfortable if measures are put in place so they can know if someone enters their room while they are asleep.

Depending on their age, a doorknob lock that they have control of can be helpful. It can also be helpful to have something like jingle bells hanging from the doorknob that will make enough noise when the door is opened so that they are not worried that they would sleep through it.

Assuming that the initial overnight visits go well, everyone has checked in with their therapists, and no one is distressed, visits can be extended, and the person can perhaps spend a weekend. Often, as the process unfolds, there is a natural opportunity. For example, during spring break or something, when it makes sense for the person who caused harm to be in the home for an extended period.

Once the person who was hurt is completely comfortable and feels very safe, the decision can be made that the person who caused harm can move back into the home. Depending on the specifics of court requirements, this may not be able to happen without approval from the probation officer or the judge, and it is important to ensure that all legal requirements are met so that no one gets in legal trouble accidentally.

If, at any point in the reunification process, anyone involved, but particularly the person who was hurt, shows signs of distress, it is important that things be slowed down or perhaps paused or stopped. Signs of distress don't always mean that reunification can't happen, though sometimes it does. Often, it means that the process is going too fast or that there is something that is happening or not happening that is worrisome for the person. There are cases when that thing is easy to figure out and fix and times when it can be more difficult, but nothing should move forward if there is any risk of harm.

One of the things abuse does is take away the victimized person's sense of power and control over their own bodies and what happens to them. It is very important that every step of healing for an abuse victim involves ensuring that they have a felt sense of control over what is happening and the decisions that are made on their behalf.

How do you know if clarification and reunification are right for you and your family and when everyone is ready?

All the reunifications I have participated in involved people who were family members. While it certainly could happen,

164

stranger abuse and/or abuse from a known person in the community usually does not result in reunification.

If the people involved are family members, particularly close family members, it is much more likely that they will want to see each other again in the future. If anyone involved does not want to participate, then it is not a good idea to move forward.

In particular, if either or both the person who got hurt and the person who caused harm are minors, then reunification should only move forward if their grown-ups are willing and supportive of the process.

What are some signs that the person who was harmed is ready to move forward with clarification and reunification?

Generally, we want the person to be able to talk about what happened to them and tolerate conversations about what happened without significant distress. I also want to see that the person's trauma symptoms have diminished and the person is feeling stable.

It is important that the individual can re-regulate and handle conversations that may cause big feelings. It is, of course, absolutely necessary that the person wants contact to occur and that they feel safe enough that contact is not detrimental to them.

How about the person who caused harm? What are the signs they are ready to participate?

The individual must be willing to acknowledge that the abuse happened and take responsibility for their behavior. They also need to be able to acknowledge the impact that their behavior has on others. They need to know that their behavior needs to stop and that changes must happen so everyone is safe. They must be able and willing to consider the needs and feelings of the person they hurt. They must be able to manage their own emotional reaction to discussions about the abuse. In addition, they must demonstrate a willingness to follow safety and family rules.

How about the parents? What are the signs they are ready for reunification to happen?

It is also important that the parents or other adults be ready to handle the process as well. Some signs of readiness include being able to acknowledge that the abuse happened and that it had an impact on the people involved. For some parents, this can be something they struggle with during their child's treatment.

The adults must also be willing to place responsibility appropriately. I have worked with families where the adults involved felt that the victim was partially responsible for what happened to them. Prior to reunification and clarification, it should hopefully have become apparent to the adults that the only person responsible for what happened was the person who committed the crime.

It is also important that the parents are able to support all the children involved and are able to manage their own emotional responses to conversations about the abuse. Parents should also, of course, be willing to follow safety rules and recommendations.

TL;DR

- Clarification and reunification are not a goal for every family, and even when it is a goal, it is not always in the best interest of everyone involved.

- There are many reasons why someone who was hurt might want to be able to see the person who hurt them again.

- It is important to ensure that everyone is ready to participate in the process and that the well-being of the person who was hurt is always kept in mind.

Key Terms in This Chapter:

Clarification letter: A structured therapeutic document wherein the offender acknowledges full responsibility for sexual abuse, expresses understanding of harm caused, and commits to preventing future abuse. (Center for Sex Offender Management (U.S.). (1999). Glossary of terms used in the management and treatment of sexual offenders. Center for Sex Offender Management. https://purl.fdlp.gov/GPO/gpo105631)

Chapter 13

Security – Making Sure Everyone is Feeling Secure and Comfortable

While ensuring "No more victims" stands as our primary treatment goal, the broader vision encompasses helping everyone build fulfilling, healthy lives. Research consistently shows that with proper treatment and support, successful community integration isn't just possible—it is the most likely outcome.

The goal of no more victims is usually not that difficult to achieve. The recidivism rate for people who have committed a sex crime, gotten caught, and received treatment is not nearly as high as the general public thinks it is. That being said, low is not the same as zero, so safety must be an important priority for everyone involved.

Parents can't supervise any child 24/7. Children go to school, attend extracurricular activities, field trips, camps, and go to friends' and relatives' homes. In addition, parents need to be able to go to the bathroom, do things around the house, and go to sleep.

There are times when a child on probation will show that they are unwilling, or unable, to follow their rules and stay safe, and also times when the adults involved are unwilling to provide supervision and follow the rules themselves. In those cases, it may not be possible for the person who caused harm to remain in the home. They may need to spend some time in a residential or locked treatment facility. Still, for the most part, it is pretty common for a person who commits a sex crime, particularly if they are a child, to be able to safely live in the community while on probation and in treatment.

Adults Who Commit Sex Crimes

Adults are, obviously, expected to be completely responsible for themselves and often don't live with their parents, though young adults are likely to still be residing at their parents' home. The specifics of what they will be required to do to ensure community safety will vary depending on the specifics of their probation rules.

Customarily, they are not allowed any contact with children and are specifically required to stay away from the person they hurt and their family. I have worked with some offenders who were allowed by the judge to have contact with children that they are related to, and occasionally, I have worked with adults who were allowed to remain in their household and parent their non-victimized children. Ordinarily, however, they are told to have no contact with any children until it is approved by their treatment provider, their probation officer, and the judge.

They are usually also required to avoid places where children gather. For example, school zones, libraries, movie theaters, theme parks, arcades, sports arenas, etc. If an adult on probation for a sex offense wishes to go to a place that would normally be off-limits, they usually need to write a safety plan and get permission from both their treatment provider and their probation officer.

Many adults choose to have someone important in their lives undergo chaperone training. If a client has a trained and approved chaperone, they are often allowed to go to some of the places in the community or attend family events that normally they would not be allowed to—as long as their chaperone is with them.

Youth Who Commit Sex Crimes

Youth do not usually have as much control over their own schedules and travel as adults do, and I have frequently worked with youth whose adults end up taking them places or putting them in positions that violate their rules and increase risk.

It is very important that any adult who will be supervising a youth with a sexual behavior problem have a good understanding of all of that youth's rules and that the adults participate in and complete chaperone training so they know how to safely supervise the youth. The individual rules and expectations for the youth will vary from jurisdiction to jurisdiction and will also be related to the specifics of the individual's needs and behavior.

In general, youth on probation for a sex crime are not usually allowed to be alone with any children who are two or more years younger than they are. If they will be around young children, it is usually important that an adult who knows about their history and has completed chaperone training be at the event.

Youth often participate in school field trips and other activities that might bring them into contact with children who are more than two years younger than them, and it is not always logistically possible, or even preferred, for their parents to attend. In those cases, youth can write a safety plan and get that approved by their treatment provider and probation officer so that they can safely attend community and school events.

Generally, once a youth has been in treatment for a little while, it is easy for the provider and probation officer to know if that is a child who will follow their rules or if the situation involves significant risk. As much as possible, it is important that youth be able to participate in typical childhood experiences. However, if that experience is something that would put the community at risk, then they will have to do more work and be willing to be safe before that would be approved.

Chaperone Training

Chaperone training is customarily offered to the loved ones of adult offenders and adults who oversee youthful offenders. Adults who want to have a chaperone usually ask a significant other or close family member to undergo the training.

Once an adult on probation has an approved chaperone, they can often get permission to attend events and locations they might not otherwise be allowed to go to. For example, an adult client with an approved chaperone may be able to attend family weddings or funerals as long as their chaperone is with them.

They may also be able to go to sporting events or other community events where children might be present.

Their ability to go will still depend on approval from their probation officer and treatment provider. I have had clients with chaperones whose probation officer still allowed very narrow privileges, but for the most part, having a chaperone makes it possible to participate in many more activities. In all the jurisdictions I have ever worked with, adults could choose to have a chaperone if they wished, but they were not required to have one, and many of my clients chose not to.

Youth on probation almost always have chaperones, at least in the jurisdictions that I have worked with. Usually, the parents of the youth on probation are required to participate in chaperone training.

I also often do chaperone training for other adults who are involved in the child's life, grandparents, aunts and uncles, and adult siblings who want to be able to take the youth with them for events or trips or who perhaps live in the home and want to be able to be an extra pair of eyes. As with adults, having a chaperone oftentimes means that youth are allowed to be involved in more activities and to attend family gatherings where young children might be present.

What does it mean to be a chaperone? It is important to note that it is not a chaperone's job to keep the other person from engaging in unsafe behavior. The choice to be safe or not to be safe is entirely and only under the control of the person on probation. If someone is determined to engage in unsafe behavior, they are the only ones responsible for that decision and their behavior.

The job of a chaperone is to be with the person whenever children (for an adult) or younger children (for an adolescent) are around. They are there as a buffer to help act as an external control and reminder to the person to follow their rules. They are also a form of protection so that the person does not get accused of doing anything that he or she did not do. Since a chaperone is usually someone that the person is close to, the person on probation can turn to them for help if they find themselves in an unsafe situation or if something happens that abruptly raises their level of risk.

For example, I had a client who attended a large family reunion, and a relative asked my client to watch her child for a few minutes while she ran to get something. Obviously, this is something that would have been a significant violation of his rules. He had his chaperone with him, who could step in and watch the child while my client moved to an area that was all adults. Similarly, I have worked with youth who have been on a family vacation and been approached by other children wherever they are, asking to play; the adults can intervene and ensure that the child on probation doesn't end up in a situation that could put them at risk of violating their rules or possibly causing harm.

Having a chaperone gives the person on probation an extra buffer and support in following their rules and dealing with the day-to-day situations that occur in the community.

After successfully completing probation and treatment, clients no longer need to write safety plans, have their chaperone with them, or get approval from their probation officer or treatment provider to travel or participate in community events. Some clients who are on the sex offender registry may still have legal restrictions and rules. If that is the case, they must familiarize themselves with the requirements of the jurisdiction they live in and any areas they travel to.

Outside of registration restrictions, however, clients who have completed their court-ordered requirements must now decide for themselves what rules they want to continue to have in their lives and what they want to let go of. Each individual and their family will need to think through what in particular would raise their individual level of risk and how they want to deal with it.

Some of my clients continue to write out safety plans for a while; some have reported to me that while they don't write them on paper, they think about the components of safety planning before going into situations. Some clients stay in touch over the years, sometimes calling to talk through their thoughts about events that are happening in their lives. What would be helpful varies from individual to individual, but it is important to talk with your treatment provider when you start approaching the end of your treatment so that you can think through what might work best for you.

Electronic Sources of Risk

I still remember a time when there was no Google, when having a computer in your home was rare, and when connecting to the internet meant you needed an available phone line along with a noisy modem and lots of spare time to wait out the slowness of the connection. Of course, now we all carry very powerful little computers in our pockets and can almost instantly access a wide array of information, images, videos, and games. In many ways, this has brought a lot of benefits to society.

However, with all that electronic power comes a great deal of risk. Children are often much more tech-savvy than adults, and the best monitoring and blocking software available still misses things. Kids are also frequently good at figuring out ways they can work around the protections their adults put in place. The easy availability of pornographic material and the wide variety of types of pornography available can have a significant impact on a person's brain and their relationship with sexuality.

Many areas of the United States have very limited sex education in schools, and children often turn to Google or other search engines to ask their questions, usually with not very helpful or healthy results. Clients on probation for a sex crime, pretty much universally, have a requirement to not view or possess pornography. For some clients, this is a fairly easy rule to follow, but for many, the desire to view pornography can become addictive in nature and difficult to avoid, even with the threat of legal consequences.

In addition to the ease of access to pornographic material, it is also very easy to connect to others, both without being honest about who you are and without really knowing who the other person is. This can easily lead to people engaging in inappropriate conversations with people whose age they are unaware of. It is not unusual for people to get themselves in legal trouble, or at best, in troubling situations, after exchanging or requesting pictures or videos that are sexual in nature.

The laws around electronic sexual behavior and children have not yet caught up to current technology. Given the pace of technological change and the usually much slower pace of legislative change, it is likely the law will always be a few steps behind. This can lead to some confusing and seemingly contradictory situations.

For example, in Texas, the legal age of consent to engage in sexual intercourse is seventeen. The child pornography laws, however, are federal, and the age of adulthood is eighteen. A seventeen-year-old person in Texas can legally consent to have a sexual relationship with another person who is seventeen or older, but if that person takes pictures or videos of themselves that are sexual in nature, they are creating child pornography and could be subject to arrest and prosecution.

Adolescents are often unaware that if they take pictures or videos of themselves that are sexual in nature, they run the risk of being prosecuted for creating child pornography. In addition, if they ask for sexual material from someone under eighteen, they can be charged with solicitation of child pornography, and if they send pictures or videos, they can get in trouble for distributing child pornography, all of which are serious crimes.

In addition to the legal implications, there are emotional consequences from exchanging intimate material with someone who may or may not keep that material private. Even when exchanged with a trusted partner, adolescents and adults should be aware that once something is in the world, there is no way to take it back, and devices and servers are often hacked on the internet. Things that people thought were private become public with regularity.

There is also the risk of pictures produced with electronic manipulation. For example, many years ago, I worked with a teenage girl whose classmates took a picture of her head and attached it to the naked body of someone else, then printed those and hung them up around the school. This was, of course, overwhelming and devastating for her, and it was difficult for her to convince the adults around her, let alone her peers, that the picture was not of her body. Unfortunately, in that case, no one was able to determine who had done that to her, and no one faced any consequences for their behavior. The girl ended up moving to a different school district in order to try and get a fresh start.

Parents must talk to their kids about what is legal and illegal in their area and also what is healthy and unhealthy. In addition, especially for children who are already on probation for a sexual offense, it is likely a good idea for parents to have monitoring software on their children's phones and other devices so that they can be alerted if the software notices something that may be problematic.

Nearly every teenager I have ever met has felt that that is an invasion of their privacy. However, it is very easy for kids to get in over their heads, even when they aren't trying to, and it is a level of protection that can be helpful. I have met some parents who monitor their children's phones secretly, and I do not recommend that, as that is a betrayal of their trust.

The best protection for youth is to have a relationship with their family where they can communicate openly, including letting the child know what decisions are being made about monitoring their devices.

When I first started working with court-ordered adults more than twenty years ago, it was typical for clients, especially adults, to have a probation restriction that banned them from using the internet and from having a phone that could access the internet or take pictures or videos.

That is a much more difficult restriction to deal with today than it was in the past. It is often not possible to apply for jobs, participate in school, deal with banking, or do most of any other aspect of day-to-day life if you do not have access to the internet.

It is also difficult to find a phone that doesn't have any of those features.

Some of my adult clients who have been on probation for a long time have found that they needed to go back to court to ask for permission to have at least limited internet access in order to work or go to school.

Of course, once someone has completed their probation, they can make their own decisions about internet access and monitoring. I have had many adult clients who feel comfortable that they can continue to live a healthy, low-risk lifestyle while having internet access; however, I have also had clients who realize that the ease of accessing sexual materials is too much of a risk for them.

For example, I worked with an adult client who got internet privileges back after not having them for over a decade. After much thought and discussion, he decided that he was uncomfortable with the level of risk he would have if he knew no one was watching. He and his adult son discussed the situation, and they agreed that monitoring and blocking software would be put on his phone and that his son would be the one who had the passwords and got the reports. This client wanted to show his son how much he had changed and continue to have a good relationship with him, his daughter-in-law, and his grandchildren. The knowledge that his son would see what he searched on the internet was enough of an external control that he felt comfortable and confident in his ability to be safe online.

Before completing treatment and probation, each individual and the family, if the individual is a minor, should talk about what they think will work best for them moving forward in life.

The Person Who Was Hurt

Sexual abuse can have a profound impact on the person who experiences it. As I have said earlier in this book, it is important that the person who was hurt is able to process their experience and hopefully work with a therapist they are comfortable with to do so.

The specific ways someone is impacted will vary from individual to individual. Some survivors of abuse get very uncomfortable with anything related to sexuality. Some survivors of abuse try to process what happened by engaging in lots of sexual and sexualized behavior. Either way, survivors of sexual abuse are often, at least for a time, more vulnerable to being in dangerous or exploitative situations.

In my experience, therapy can help mitigate those effects, but it is not always something that gets resolved quickly or easily. It is important that the person who was hurt has adults in their life who are comfortable discussing sex and sexuality openly and that they know they can bring any concerns or troubles to them without being judged.

Survivors of abuse often get hurtful and inaccurate messages from society. More than one woman who was sexually abused as a child has told me that somewhere along the way, a doctor, therapist, or sometimes even a friend or family member has told them that they should stay away from kids or not have children because now that they were abused, they are likely to abuse others. That is not based on any actual science, but it is the type of statement that stays with a person and makes them fearful of themselves.

Children who were abused nearly always convince themselves, sadly, sometimes with the help of the people around them, that they are responsible for what happened to them. That is also complete nonsense, of course. The only person responsible for abuse is the person who did the abusing.

In addition, I have often worked with both children and adults who were abused as children who feel responsible for the adults in their lives being stressed or sad or for their family structure changing. People who feel badly about themselves or feel they are somehow broken or damaged can find themselves in situations that cause them further harm, often because they don't believe they truly deserve better.

Parents of children who have been victimized must reassure them, often repeatedly, that they are not at fault, that they are not broken or problematic, and that they are wonderful humans deserving of dignity, respect, and love.

TL;DR

- "No more victims" is an important underlying goal of therapy.

- Chaperone training can help the loved ones of someone who caused harm to know how to help that person stay safe.

- It is important to think about what each person involved needs in order to be and feel safe.

Key Terms in This Chapter:

Electronic monitoring: Digital supervision tools used to track and restrict online activities. (National Institute of Justice, "Sex Offender Management Assessment and Planning Initiative," 2023)

Chapter 14

Thrive – Looking to the Future

The stories you're about to read represent hope, resilience, and the real possibility of healing after sexual abuse. Each narrative comes from someone who has walked this difficult path and emerged stronger, wiser, and ready to help others understand that recovery is possible.

This isn't an easy topic, and there is a lot in this book that can feel heavy or overwhelming. Hopefully, most of your questions have been answered, and your concerns have been addressed. If some have not, I hope you have at least gotten ideas about resources you can contact for information about your situation. I also hope that throughout the book, I have made it clear that while this is a serious issue that takes lots of time and attention and creates stress, there is also hope and the knowledge that there is every possibility that the future is likely to go well.

I thought it might be useful to end this book with some stories from folks who have been through the process and, with the benefit of hindsight, can let you know what the experience was like for them. As always, identifying details have been changed, and client stories represent a combination of a number of people rather than any specific individuals.

Thoughts from a teenage girl who experienced a lot of trauma from various sources and had multiple therapists in the past.

I told everyone who would listen that I didn't need or want to talk to a therapist. Even before my brother did what he did, the therapists that I saw didn't help, and the ones I saw after just told me I had too many problems to fix and that they couldn't help me. I knew that I have always and will always handle my own problems myself. No one else cares anyway, so why should I? I remember when I first started having to see you, I did everything I could to avoid talking to you. I also tried being mean and loud for a while. Do you remember when I used to come in and just yell and swear the whole time? I can't believe you didn't kick me out. I was sure you would decide I had too many problems, just like the other therapist I saw, or maybe just disappear like a different one did. When yelling didn't work, I tried just sitting silently, but that didn't work either, and I'm not good at being quiet anyway. It has been several years now. I was still in elementary school when I met you, and now I am in high school. I never managed to get you to kick me out, and after a while, I didn't really want you to. It started to seem maybe a little helpful to have somewhere to go where I could be mad or sad or loud or quiet and not get into trouble or have anyone tell me I was bothering them. I still think I can handle my own problems myself, even if sometimes talking to you about them is helpful. I have pretty much stopped getting into trouble at school. They let me back out of the school for kids with problems, and I am back in the regular school now. I haven't even gotten detention for anything yet this school year, which is kind of weird. I got to see my brother again; that was awkward, and he feels like a stranger, but maybe I'll get a chance to get to know him again now. I know I don't need you, and I can handle things myself. I'm only coming because my mom makes me, but it is nice to know I can talk to you, and you seem to like me even when the other adults in my life don't.

If I were going to give advice to a kid who is going through what I went through, I would say, try not to let other people make you feel bad. Sometimes, people will hurt you or treat you badly, but really, that is their problem. Hold your head up and remember that no one else gets to tell you who you are. Some people just suck; that isn't your fault. Don't be afraid to tell people what happened, and no one should get to hurt you. If I were giving advice to parents, I would say don't ignore red flags or sweep things under the rug. My parents told me they had seen some things that made them wonder if something was happening but ignored them for a while. If you think something might be happening, ask the kid. Also, adults shouldn't expect kids to act like nothing happened. I get in trouble sometimes because I have been angry. I have anger issues for a reason. Why wouldn't I be angry? I don't know if any other therapists will read your book, but if they do, I have advice for them, too. Don't give up on kids. If you are going to be a therapist, don't say no to kids who need you.

Thoughts from a teenager who abused his younger sibling

I remember when my parents realized what was happening. It was scary, but I'm really glad because I kept telling myself I would stop and then I would do it again. I haven't done anything like that since I got caught and since I went to treatment. I know what to do if I ever think about doing something like that again. I haven't had thoughts like those in a long time, though. I used to feel like a monster, like I should be kept away from everyone and no one should ever talk to me. My therapists told me that staying away from everyone and not talking to anyone at school wasn't good for me, but in the beginning, I just wanted to hide and sleep and maybe disappear. I knew I needed to do things differently, and therapy helped, even though it was really hard, and a lot of times I just wanted to avoid it. It took a while, but eventually, I started being honest, not just about what I did but also about how I felt and what I was thinking. I talked about things I promised myself I would never tell anyone. It turns out my therapist wasn't lying to me, and once I talked about those things, I really did feel better, not worse like I thought I would. Writing the letter to my younger brother was really hard, and I was very scared about seeing him again. I don't know why he doesn't hate me, but he doesn't seem to. Nowadays, we play video games together, and I get to act like a big brother should. He knows I won't hurt him again and that I will do whatever I need to so that he feels safe.

If I were giving advice to another kid who just got on probation, I would say it will be okay. It is hard, but try to be honest as soon as you can—it really did make everything go better. You aren't a monster. You need to learn how to handle things differently and manage your sexual behavior so you are safe and healthy. I didn't think my parents or brother would forgive me, but they did, and that seemed to happen for all the other kids I met in treatment, so it will probably happen for you, too. You deserve to be safe and happy—be honest and take responsibility for what you did and you will be.

Thoughts from a child who was abused by her father

If I were talking to someone who experienced what I experienced, I would say it is rough at first, but it does get better. In the beginning, I felt really guilty. My dad had sexually abused me, not my siblings. He wasn't always very nice to my younger siblings, but at the time, we all thought that was just how dads were. I felt like it was my fault that my younger siblings didn't have a dad, that if I had kept quiet about what he was doing or maybe found a different way to stop him, he would still be at home with us. After a while, I was able to see that not having him with us was a good thing. Not only am I safe from being abused, but also my siblings are safe from the possibility of him doing that to them when they get older. He told me that if I let him do it to me, he would leave them alone, but he lied a lot, so maybe he would have eventually done it to them, too. I know now I could not have found a different way to stop him. He kept promising me he would stop, but that never lasted very long. Now we are all safe.

When my dad left, I was really worried about my younger siblings and worried that my mom would be overwhelmed, so I tried to be an extra mom to them for a while. It helped when my mom would remind me that it wasn't my job.

If there are any parents reading this, I would advise that they make sure to tell their kid that they should be a kid, not an adult, especially since I lost a lot of my early childhood because of the abuse. I'm pretty mature, but sometimes I act younger than my age, and it would be helpful if all the adults around me realized that was because I didn't get to be a little kid when I was one. I would also tell the adults to find their kid a therapist who can be around for a while. My first therapist worked at a place that only let clients stay in therapy for a few months. It felt really bad when I had to change. My second therapist didn't have time restrictions, and I have seen her for several years. I don't see her that often anymore, but I know if something bothers me or if I start thinking about the things my dad did to me or showed me, I can talk to her about it, and that helps it be less of a problem. Now, I can focus on school and extracurricular activities and hanging out with my best friend. I still worry about my siblings, but I know my mom can take care of all of us, and I can just be a big sister and not an extra mom, at least most of the time. My dad will be in prison for a long time. His first chance of parole doesn't happen until all of us kids are adults. I don't know if I want to talk to him again in the future. I kind of want to tell him off and make sure he knows how bad he hurt me, but I know I don't have to worry about deciding about that for a long time.

My family is doing well now. In the beginning, I wasn't sure we would be okay again, but we are. It was hard and scary, but don't worry, things will get better. Don't be afraid; what happened wasn't your fault, and you deserve to be safe.

Thoughts from a parent whose older child abused their younger sibling

It felt like a nightmare. When I realized what was happening, I almost couldn't believe it. There are no words to describe how scary and overwhelming it was. We knew the right thing was to make sure it was reported, which we did, but it was terrifying. Separating the kids was hard. Luckily, my parents were able to help for a while, and we were able to manage to keep them away from each other until our daughter felt okay seeing him, and the therapists told us it would be okay. It was sometimes hard to support everyone, especially when our oldest would have a setback or would do something he wasn't supposed to, like go look at pornography. He caused his sister so much hurt, and it was hard to be a good parent to him while we were so angry.

It was hard to find time, but if someone just starting to go through this asked me for advice, I would say to find someone you can talk to also. It's too hard to try and figure everything out on your own, and it's too overwhelming to try to manage without someone who can help. I had friends and family to talk to also, but that was different than talking to a therapist who has seen other people who have gone through this before. In the beginning, I wasn't sure things would ever be okay again. It's been a while now, and we are all back together again in one house. We were able to set up safety things so my daughter wasn't worried, and we would know if our son was not following the rules. All the kids have started focusing more on other things, and the abuse isn't the focus of our lives anymore. It comes up sometimes in therapy, but the kids are usually more focused on what is going on at school and with their peers. It does get better. Find professionals you trust, advocate for your kids, and don't ignore your own mental health. Time doesn't heal things, but time plus a lot of hard work has worked for us.

Thoughts from a mom whose husband abused their child and is incarcerated

You will survive this. I know it doesn't feel like it, but you will. Protect your kids and everything else will eventually be okay, too. Lean on your tribe; my friends and family are the reason we are doing well now. Also, expand your tribe and find therapists who know what they are doing and can help. If the professionals aren't helping, find new ones. None of my kids are with the first therapist we found. Sometimes, it was because of time limits, and sometimes, it was because it wasn't a good fit. Don't be afraid to advocate for your kids. We even changed pediatricians because one was dismissive of my daughter's feelings. It is important that my kids know I will always advocate for them and keep them safe. If I could go back in time, I would have asked more questions. I would have asked the people to slow down and explain things to me and let both the kids and me know what was happening. I wish there had been a checklist or something because sometimes I didn't know what to do next. When my daughter told me what was happening, we went to the police station that night. They had me come back the next day with all the kids to the Child Advocacy Center. At the time, I didn't know what that was or what would happen there. It was overwhelming. They kept giving me paperwork to fill out, and I'm not even sure what all I signed. They took the kids and had them strip to do the medical exam. I didn't know that was going to happen. In between paperwork, they would pull me into rooms with each kid so I could be with them during the medical exam. I am very grateful I could be there to support them, but no one warned me or explained what would be happening, and it was totally overwhelming. They also interviewed all the kids, questioned me, and then sent us home. Once we got home, I had no idea what to do next. It was overwhelming and traumatic for all of us, and I felt paralyzed; a list of things to do would have helped a lot. That was years ago. We have found our way, and you will, too. Don't be afraid to ask for and accept help. You will get through this. I would never have imagined how good things would end up being. That will happen for you, too.

Thoughts from a mom whose husband abused her child and whose family was able to reunify

The period of time just after I learned about the abuse was the most overwhelming time in my life. It is hard to trust your own gut because your world just got upended, but it is also important to trust yourself because you know your kids the best and have their best interests at heart. In my case, nearly everyone else, the DA (district attorney), the victim services people, CPS (Child Protective Services), all had their own agenda. Some were a little helpful, some were not helpful at all, but I never felt like any of them were truly on my or my kids' side. Some things felt like no-win situations. For example, early on, I told the DA that I wanted to kill my husband, and he told me that he would charge me with threatening to murder someone. At another meeting, I told him that I wanted my husband to stay out of jail so he could continue to work and help pay for all the things the kids need. When I said that, he told me I wasn't being a protective parent and that I might have the kids taken away from me. No matter how I reacted, I was told I wasn't reacting correctly. The only initial professional who provided us with any comfort was the CPS caseworker, who told me she didn't want to take my kids and that as long as I made sure there was no contact between them and him, they would get to stay with me. That was a relief to hear, and she was the only person who didn't make the process antagonistic. It has been over a decade since the abuse came to light, and many things have changed.

If I were to give advice to someone who just started this process, I'm not even sure I would tell them to follow the path we did.

With the help of a lot of work from everyone involved, as well as teams of therapists, our family has stayed together. I know, though, that reunification is not always possible, and a lot of things came together to make it work for us. My husband has completed all his requirements, and we are living together again. Our children, who are now adults, have reconciled with him, and neither of them is uncomfortable around him anymore. That only happened, however, because everyone involved, my husband included, was willing to do the hard work to make it happen. I know from talking to the therapists we have worked with that lots of families do reunify, but I know lots do not. It was the right decision for my kids, but I know it is not the right decision for everyone. Whatever the outcome is for your family, I would say find the people who bring you comfort and are helpful.

Advocate for your kids. You are the one who knows them best. Find a therapist outside the system. Having a therapist my daughter liked, who was not a part of the criminal justice system and was willing to advocate for her and testify in court if needed, made a big difference. In the end, we had, and still have, multiple therapists helping to support our family. My husband did his court-ordered treatment with the therapist he was assigned to by probation, and he continues to see her occasionally to check in and talk about what is currently going on in his life. Both my children have had therapists, but as they have grown, they have changed providers a few times. I have had my own individual therapist and have also changed providers over time. It can be difficult to find someone who doesn't react poorly to finding out my husband committed a sex offense, and I would definitely advise finding therapists who are familiar with this kind of work. My husband and I also see a couple's counselor every few months, and we have all done family therapy together in the past. It has been a lot of time, effort, uncertainty, and stress. In the beginning, I didn't know if I wanted to stay with him or if I could ever not be ragingly angry at him. I didn't know if staying with him would be good for the kids or if it would feel like a betrayal to them. In the end, all of us are glad we stayed together, but it was a long and winding road. Finding good therapists is the reason we made it. Don't be afraid to shop around, and if a particular therapist is not a good fit, find someone else.

Thoughts from a juvenile probation officer who has twenty years experience working with youth who have committed sex crimes and their families.

When I first meet with families, they are usually pretty overwhelmed and scared. They are afraid of what the future holds and what being on probation will be like for their child. Lots of parents have told me they don't think that their child needs to, or should, participate in treatment. If your child had a medical problem, like cancer, you would want them to get the help they need, and this is the same thing. Ignoring the problem won't help. Children who commit sex crimes need treatment. It is important for them to address whatever has led them to commit the crime and make sure they are safe and healthy so they can live the rest of their lives without worry or causing harm.

It is also important for parents to know that this is a journey; it will take a while, and your child will probably mess up and break some of their rules at some point. They can still move forward and be successful, even if there are some difficulties along the way. My job is to enforce the rules and legal requirements, so sometimes it can seem like I am the enemy, but ideally, there will be a good working relationship between the probation officer and the treatment provider, and we work together to help your child succeed. You, the parent, make a very valuable addition to creating an effective treatment team for your child.

Don't be afraid to advocate for your child. If something feels off or wrong, say something. Ask questions; there are no stupid questions. I would much rather you ask as many questions as you need to understand the requirements rather than guess and end up in legal trouble. We are here to be a resource and support to help your child and you successfully meet all their probation requirements so they can heal and move into their futures. The vast majority of youth on probation for a sex offense that I have worked with are able to successfully complete probation and move on with their lives. Parental involvement and support make a huge difference for everyone involved.

Key Terms in This Chapter:

Post-treatment success: Sustained positive outcomes following completion of sexual offense treatment, including no new offenses and healthy community reintegration (U.S. Department of Justice's research on treatment outcomes in sex offense cases, 2023)

Recovery process: The dynamic journey of healing from sexual abuse trauma through therapeutic intervention and support systems. (American Psychological Association's guidelines for therapists treating trauma patients, 2024)

Resilience: The capacity to adapt positively and maintain psychological well-being despite experiencing sexual abuse trauma. (The National Child Traumatic Stress Network, the leading U.S. organization studying childhood trauma, 2023)

Glossary of Terms

A

Adjudication: The formal giving or pronouncing of a judgment in a legal proceeding. (*Legal Dictionary*)

Adolescent offenders: Minors who commit criminal acts or engage in delinquent behavior. (Office of Juvenile Justice and Delinquency Prevention, 2020)

Aftercare: Continued outpatient treatment following completion of residential treatment. (National Institute on Drug Abuse (NIDA), "Principles of Drug Addiction Treatment," 2018)

Allostasis: Process of maintaining stability through physiological or behavioral change. (McEwen, *Hormones and Behavior Journal*, "The Concept of Allostasis")

Amygdala: Brain structure responsible for detecting and responding to threats. (AbuHasan Q, Reddy V, Siddiqui W. (2023). Neuroanatomy, Amygdala. StatPearls Publishing; https://www.ncbi.nlm.nih.gov/books/NBK537102/)

C

Center for Disease Control (CDC): The national public health agency of the United States responsible for disease control and prevention. (Centers for Disease Control and Prevention, 2023)

Chaperone: A person responsible for monitoring interactions to ensure safety. (Association for the Treatment and Prevention of Sexual Abuse (ATSA), "Practice Guidelines for the

Assessment, Treatment, and Management of Male Adult Sexual Abusers," 2014)

Chaperone training: Specialized training for approved adults who supervise offenders in community settings. "Community Supervision Protocols," (Center for Sex Offender Management, 2021)

Child advocacy center: A facility designed to provide a child-friendly, safe environment for forensic interviews and services for children who may have experienced abuse. (National Children's Alliance definition)

Child Protective Services (CPS): A government agency responsible for investigating child abuse and neglect reports and providing services to at-risk families. (U.S. Department of Health & Human Services, Administration for Children & Families. Child Protective Services. https://www.childwelfare.gov/topics/responding/cps/)

Clarification: A therapeutic process where the person who caused harm takes responsibility and communicates this to the person they hurt (Center for Sex Offender Management (U.S.). (1999). Glossary of terms used in the management and treatment of sexual offenders. Center for Sex Offender Management. https://purl.fdlp.gov/GPO/gpo105631)

Clarification letter: A structured therapeutic document wherein the offender acknowledges full responsibility for sexual abuse, expresses understanding of harm caused, and commits to preventing future abuse. (Center for Sex Offender Management (U.S.). (1999). Glossary of terms used in the management and treatment of sexual offenders. Center for Sex Offender Management. https://purl.fdlp.gov/GPO/gpo105631)

Court-ordered treatment: Mandatory therapy or counseling required by legal authority. (Legal/Clinical composite definition)

D

Denial: A psychological defense mechanism in which a person refuses to accept reality or facts. (American Psychological Association)

Diaphragmatic breathing: Deep breathing technique engaging the diaphragm muscle. (Hamasaki H. (2020). Effects of Diaphragmatic Breathing on Health: A Narrative Review. Medicines (Basel, Switzerland), 7(10), 65. https://doi.org/10.3390/medicines7100065)

Dynamic risk factors: Characteristics or circumstances that can change over time and may affect the likelihood of reoffending. (Andrews & Bonta, 2010)

E

Electronic monitoring: Digital supervision tools used to track and restrict online activities. (National Institute of Justice (2023), "Sex Offender Management Assessment and Planning Initiative")

EMDR (Eye Movement Desensitization and Reprocessing): Trauma therapy technique using bilateral stimulation to process difficult memories. (EMDR International Association)

F

False accusations: Untrue allegations of abuse or misconduct, which are statistically rare in child abuse cases. (Oates et al., *Child Abuse & Neglect*, 2000)

Fight/flight/freeze response: Automatic physiological reaction to perceived harmful events or threats. (*Harvard Review of Psychiatry*, "Fear and the Defense Cascade")

Forensic interview: A structured conversation with a child conducted by a trained professional to gather information about possible abuse or neglect. (National Children's Advocacy Center, 2019)

Foster care: A system in which a minor is placed into a ward, group home, or private home of a state-certified caregiver. (Child Welfare Information Gateway, 2021)

G

Good Lives Model: Strengths-based rehabilitation framework focusing on building capabilities for a fulfilling life. (Ward & Brown, 2004)

GPS ankle monitor: Electronic device used to track an individual's location as part of legal supervision (Department of Justice definition)

Grounding: Therapeutic technique connecting one physically or mentally to the present moment. (van der Kolk, *The Body Keeps the Score*)

H

Healing: The process of becoming healthy or whole again after physical or emotional trauma. (*Merriam-Webster*)

Homeostasis: The body's tendency to maintain internal stability and balance. (Cannon, *The Wisdom of the Body*)

I

Inappropriate sexual behavior: Sexual actions that are considered improper, unsuitable, or violate social norms or laws. (National Center on the Sexual Behavior of Youth, 2022)

Internal Family Systems (IFS): Therapeutic paradigm that views every human as a system of protective and wounded inner parts led by a core self. (IFS Institute)

Intervention: An action taken to improve a situation or prevent it from getting worse. (*Oxford Languages*)

L

Law enforcement: The system of people and organizations that ensures obedience to the law. (Cambridge Dictionary)

Legal privilege: Legal protection that keeps certain communications confidential. (American Bar Association)

Licensed sex offender treatment provider: A mental health professional with specialized training and certification to treat individuals who have committed sexual offenses. (Texas Department of State Health Services)

Locked treatment facility: A secure care setting where residents' movements and access to the community are restricted. (California Department of Social Services, 2022)

M

Multigenerational abuse: A pattern of maltreatment that is passed down from one generation to the next within a family. (Child Welfare Information Gateway, 2016)

Multigenerational trauma: Trauma patterns passed down through family generations. (van der Kolk, *The Body Keeps the Score*)

N

Nervous system: The complex of nerve tissues that control the activities of the body. (*Merriam-Webster*)

Nervous system regulation: Process of managing and balancing autonomic nervous system responses. (Porges, *The Polyvagal Theory*)

Non-offending parent: A parent who did not participate in the abuse of their child and may or may not have been aware that the abuse was occurring. (National Children's Alliance, 2022)

O

Outcry: A disclosure or report of abuse, typically made by a victim. (Texas Department of Family and Protective Services)

Outcry of abuse: The first verbal statement about abuse made by a victim to another person. (Texas Department of Family and Protective Services, 2018)

Outpatient treatment: Therapeutic services provided while the client lives at home. (Healthcare definition)

P

Parasympathetic nervous system (PNS): Part of the autonomic nervous system responsible for "rest and digest" functions. (Tortora & Derrickson, *Principles of Anatomy and Physiology*)

Perpetrators: Individuals who commit harmful or illegal acts against others. (*Merriam-Webster*)

Plea deal: A legal agreement between defendant and prosecutor to resolve a case without trial. (*Black's Law Dictionary*)

Polygraph exam: A procedure that measures and records several physiological indicators while a person answers questions. (American Polygraph Association)

Post-adjudication assessment: Evaluation conducted after legal proceedings to assess treatment progress. (Legal/Clinical composite definition)

Post-traumatic stress disorder (PTSD): A psychiatric disorder that may occur after experiencing or witnessing a traumatic event. (American Psychiatric Association, DSM-5)

Post-treatment success: Sustained positive outcomes following completion of sexual offense treatment, including no new offenses and healthy community reintegration. (U.S. Department of Justice's research on treatment outcomes in sex offense cases, 2023)

Pre-adjudication assessment: Evaluation conducted before legal proceedings to assess risk and treatment needs. (Legal/Clinical composite definition)

Pre-sentencing assessment: Evaluation conducted after conviction but before sentencing to inform court decisions about appropriate consequences. (Legal/Clinical composite definition)

Probation: A sentencing option in which instead of incarcerating an individual, the court releases the person to the community and orders them to complete a period of supervision monitored by a probation officer while abiding by certain conditions.

Probation staffing meetings: Regular meetings of the multidisciplinary team, including probation officers, treatment providers, and other professionals collaborating to monitor and support the progress of the client in court-ordered treatment and their families.

Protective parent: A parent who takes appropriate action to protect their child from harm. (American Professional Society on the Abuse of Children, 2017)

Psychoeducation: Educational intervention providing information about mental health conditions and treatment. (*APA Dictionary of Psychology*)

R

Recidivism rate: The likelihood of a person reoffending or engaging in criminal behavior after receiving intervention or punishment. (U.S. Department of Justice, 2014)

Recovery process: The dynamic journey of healing from sexual abuse trauma through therapeutic intervention and support systems. (American Psychological Association, 2024)

Residential treatment: Intensive treatment program where the client lives at the facility. (American Academy of Child and Adolescent Psychiatry, 2010)

Resilience: The capacity to adapt positively and maintain psychological well-being despite experiencing sexual abuse trauma. (The National Child Traumatic Stress Network, 2023)

Resiliency: The process of adapting well in the face of adversity, trauma, tragedy, threats, or significant sources of stress. (American Psychological Association)

Reunification: A clinical process facilitating safe contact between a sexual abuse victim and offender, typically within families, following thorough assessment and preparation of all parties. (Association for the Treatment and Prevention of Sexual Abuse, 2022)

Risk assessment: Structured evaluation to determine the likelihood of future problematic behavior. (Association for the Treatment and Prevention of Sexual Abuse)

S

Safety plan: Document required for special events outlining behavioral guidelines and boundaries. (Beacon, Dr. Nicolas Carrasco)

Safety rules: Specific guidelines put in place to prevent further abuse and protect vulnerable individuals. (Center for Sex Offender Management, 2008)

SANE (Sexual Assault Nurse Examiner) exam: A medical examination performed by a specially trained nurse to collect evidence and provide care following a sexual assault. (International Association of Forensic Nurses)

Sand tray therapy: Expressive therapy technique using miniatures and sand for nonverbal processing. (Association for Play Therapy)

Sex crime: A criminal offense involving illegal or coerced sexual conduct against another person. (Legal Information Institute, Cornell Law School)

Sexual abuse: Unwanted sexual activity, often involving physical contact, perpetrated against a person who cannot or does not give consent. (American Psychological Association)

Sexual behavior problems: Developmentally inappropriate or intrusive sexual behaviors that may cause harm to self or others. (Association for the Treatment and Prevention of Sexual Abuse)

Sexual education: A teaching about human sexuality, including intimate relationships, human sexual anatomy, sexual reproduction, sexually transmitted infections, sexual activity, sexual orientation, gender identity, abstinence, contraception, and reproductive rights and responsibilities. (Planned Parenthood)

Somatic experiencing: Body-focused trauma therapy approach addressing physical and emotional trauma symptoms. (Somatic Experiencing International)

Static risk factors: Historical or unchangeable factors used to assess risk of future behavior. (Andrews & Bonta, 2010)

Stranger abuse: Sexual abuse perpetrated by someone unknown to the victim. (RAINN)

Stranger danger: The warning about the risks associated with trusting or interacting with strangers. (*Oxford Learner's Dictionaries*)

Stress response: The body's reaction to any change requiring adjustment or adaptation. (Sapolsky, *Why Zebras Don't Get Ulcers*)

Survivors: Individuals who have lived through a traumatic experience, such as sexual abuse. (RAINN)

Sympathetic nervous system (SNS): Part of the autonomic nervous system that activates the "fight or flight" response. *(Marieb, E. N., & Hoehn, K. (2022). Human anatomy and physiology (12th global ed.). Pearson.)*

T

Therapeutic relationship: The working alliance between therapist and client that facilitates healing and change. (*APA Dictionary of Psychology*)

Theraplay: Attachment-based therapeutic approach focusing on parent-child relationships. (The Theraplay Institute)

Trauma: An emotional response to a terrible event like an accident, rape, or natural disaster. (American Psychological Association)

Trauma response: Physical and emotional reactions to traumatic events. (International Society for Traumatic Stress Studies)

Traumatic sexual behavior: Sexual behaviors that are developmentally inappropriate, coercive, or potentially harmful, often exhibited by children or adolescents. (National Center on the Sexual Behavior of Youth)

Treatment manual: Structured guide for therapeutic intervention containing specific assignments and measures of progress that provide a framework for treatment delivery. (Clinical practice definition)

Treatment plan: A structured plan developed for a specific client's treatment goals. (Clinical practice definition)

Treatment provider: Professional responsible for delivering therapeutic services and establishing treatment-specific rules.

Treatment team: A multidisciplinary group of professionals who work together to provide services for a client.

V

Victimize: To subject someone to deception, duress, or other criminal activity. (*Oxford Languages*)

Victimized person: An individual who has suffered direct or threatened physical, emotional, or pecuniary (financial) harm as a result of the commission of a crime. (U.S. Department of Justice, 2021)

W

Well-functioning family: A family unit that effectively manages stress, communicates openly, and supports individual growth. (Family Process Institute, 2021)

Work product: Materials prepared by or for an attorney in preparation for litigation. (*Black's Law Dictionary*)

Y

Youth with sexual behavior problems: Minors who engage in inappropriate or harmful sexual behaviors toward others. (Association for the Treatment and Prevention of Sexual Abusers, 2022)

Bibliography

AbuHasan Q, Reddy V, Siddiqui W. (2023). Neuroanatomy, Amygdala. StatPearls Publishing; https://www.ncbi.nlm.nih.gov/ books/NBK537102/

American Bar Association. *Standards for Criminal Justice: Confidential Communications and Legal Privilege* (4th ed.). pp. 127-156. ABA Publishing, 2024. Association for Treatment of Sexual Abusers. *Practice Guidelines for Assessment, Treatment, and Management of Adults with Sexual Behavior Problems. ATSA Professional Standards and Guidelines Series, Volume 3*. pp. 45-89. ATSA, 2024.

Bureau of Justice Statistics. Measuring Recidivism in Sexual Offender Populations: Technical and Methodological Standards (Report No. NCJ-302947), pp. 1-42. U.S. Department of Justice, 2024.

Center for Sex Offender Management. Community Supervision Protocols for Sex Offender Management (4th ed.). Report NCJ-238264. pp. 132-189. Office of Justice Programs, U.S. Department of Justice, 2021.

Center for Sex Offender Management (U.S.). (1999). Glossary of terms used in the management and treatment of sexual offenders. Center for Sex Offender Management. https://purl.fdlp.gov/GPO/gpo105631

Child Welfare Information Gateway. Family Reunification: What the Evidence Shows (Report HHS-2023-ACF-ACYF-CA-0080), pp. 1-76. U.S. Department of Health and Human Services, 2023.

Duncan, S. *Treatment for Youth with Sexual Behavior Problems: A Practical Guide for Identifying Treatment Programs That Empower Clients and Transform Lives.* Laughing Rock, 2023.

Finkelhor, D., Ormrod, R., & Chaffin, M. "Juveniles who commit sex offenses against minors." *Juvenile Justice Bulletin,* NCJ227763. US Government Printing Office, 2009.

Fortson, B. L., Klevens, J., Merrick, M. T., Gilbert, L. K., & Alexander, S. P. "Child Abuse and Neglect Prevention Resource for Action: A Compilation of the Best Available Evidence." National Center for Injury Prevention and Control, Centers for Disease Control and Prevention, 2016.

Goulston, M. *Just Listen: Discover the Secret to Getting Through to Absolutely Anyone.* American Management Association, 2010.

Hamasaki H. (2020). Effects of Diaphragmatic Breathing on Health: A Narrative Review. Medicines (Basel, Switzerland), 7(10), 65. https://doi.org/10.3390/medicines7100065

International Society for Traumatic Stress Studies. *Clinical Handbook of Trauma Response and Treatment (3rd ed.),* pp. 89-127. Guilford Press, 2024.

Marieb, E. N., & Hoehn, K. (2022). Human anatomy and physiology (12th global ed.). Pearson.

National Center on Sexual Behavior of Youth. (2024). Treatment Manual for Youth with Sexual Behavior Problems (Vol. 2). University of Oklahoma Health Sciences Center. Report NCSBY-2024-01, pp. 1-156.

National Children's Advocacy Center. *Forensic Interviewing Protocol (5th ed.)*, pp. 23-67. NCAC Training Series, 2023. https://www.michigan.gov/mdhhs/-/media/Project/Websites/mdhhs/Adult-and-Childrens-Services/Abuse-and-Neglect/Childrens-Protective-Services/DHS-PUB-0779-Fifth-Edition.pdf?rev=ea6f15c43426455281f1b6eca73c88fc&hash=0C48241F7B09473C4F98A2D65BE53BF9

Porges, S. *The Polyvagal Theory in Clinical Practice* (2nd ed.), pp. 45-203.

W.W. Norton & Company, 2023.

Safer Society Foundation. *Treatment Program Guidelines for Sexual Behavior Problems*. 4. pp. 89-156. Clinical Practice Series, 2023.

Sapolsky, R. *Why Zebras Don't Get Ulcers. 3rd ed.* Holt Paperbacks, 2004.

Siegel, D. J., & Payne Bryson, T. *The Whole-Brain Child: 12 Revolutionary Strategies to Nurture Your Child's Developing Mind*. Bantum, 2012.

Snyder, H. N. Sexual assault of young children as reported to law enforcement: Victim, incident, and offender characteristics: A statistical report using data from the national incident-based reporting system. US Department of Justice, Office of Justice Programs, Bureau of Justice Statistics, 2000.

Tortora, G. J., & Derrickson, B. H. *Principles of Anatomy and Physiology (16th ed.)*, pp. 578-612. John Wiley & Sons.

van der Kolk, B. *The Body Keeps the Score: Brain, Mind, and Body in the Healing of Trauma*, pp. 166-204. Penguin Books, 2015

Dedication & Acknowledgments

Like all books, this one would not have been possible without the support and help from the people around me, both in my personal and professional life.

I wish to thank my colleagues whose unwavering dedication to supporting the health, well-being, and healing of our fellow humans is an inspiration.

In addition, I wish to thank all the members of the twelve-week book writing group. I don't write nearly as fast as some of the rest of you, but my writing journey would not have been possible without the community that we have created.

I had the great benefit of editing and proofreading from both Tamelynda Lux and Ita de Groot. Any mistakes are my own, but there would be a lot more of them without their professionalism and dedication to detail.

I also appreciate the support of my friends and family who are, by now, quite used to me disappearing to write for large blocks of time. Thank you so much for putting up with my need to sometimes disconnect.

Underlying everything else, this book is dedicated to all my clients. Choosing to face pain and trauma and be open to healing is an act of incredible courage, and I have been honored beyond measure to be a part of your journey.

About the Author

Dr. Shanti Duncan is a Licensed Professional Counselor (LPC) and Licensed Sex Offender Treatment Provider (LSOTP) in private practice in Central Texas. She has extensive experience working with people who have experienced trauma and with youth and adults with sexual behavior problems. She is the author of *Treatment for Youth with Sexual Behavior Problems*.

Dr. Duncan lives with her husband, children, dogs, cats, and a tortoise. When not working or spending time with family, Dr. Duncan enjoys gardening, reading, and playing music with others.

Shanti Duncan is available for speaking engagements.

For details, please connect with her at:

12407 North Mopac Expwy Ste 250-285

Austin, TX 78758-2475

Shanti.duncan.lpc@gmail.com